Jessica Alba's Honest Success:
Building a Health and Wellness Empire

Introduction

In a world dominated by fast-paced consumerism and relentless celebrity culture, few stories stand out as testaments to genuine, impactful change. Jessica Alba's journey from Hollywood A-lister to the founder of The Honest Company is one of those rare transformations. Known initially as a magnetic star on screen, Alba has redefined herself beyond the red carpet and magazine covers, emerging as a businesswoman with a purpose-driven mission: to make clean, sustainable products accessible to all families.

Jessica's story is about far more than simply putting her name on a product line. From the beginning, she was determined to create an honest brand that challenged industry standards. Her motivation was deeply personal. As a new mother navigating her own health sensitivities, Jessica became acutely aware of the potential toxins in everyday products—from lotions to household cleaners. Frustrated by the lack of transparency and safe options on the market, she took matters into her own hands, vowing to create products that were not only safe but also affordable, beautifully designed, and accessible to families across the globe.

This journey wasn't without obstacles. When Alba first entered the business world, skeptics questioned her intentions and commitment. After all, celebrity endorsements often don't extend beyond a photo shoot or two. But Jessica defied expectations, immersing herself in every aspect of The Honest Company, from product development to ethical sourcing, and even personally researching non-toxic ingredients. She wanted her company to stand for more than just profits; it had to stand for trust, transparency, and an unwavering dedication to quality.

Jessica Alba's Honest Success: Building a Health and Wellness Empire tells the remarkable story of how Jessica's vision and resilience turned her into a pioneering entrepreneur and her brand into a leader in the health and wellness industry. Her journey is a masterclass in breaking stereotypes, staying true to one's mission, and building a brand that people can genuinely believe in. From humble beginnings to billion-dollar success, Alba's path reveals the power of authenticity and purpose in a world where both can be hard to come by.

This book delves into the key lessons and defining moments that have shaped Jessica Alba and The Honest Company. Whether you're an aspiring entrepreneur, a business enthusiast, or simply curious about the evolution of one of Hollywood's most successful crossovers, you'll find inspiration and actionable insights within these pages. Alba's commitment to quality and her journey to make the world a safer place for families and children is not just her story—it's a blueprint for anyone looking to build something meaningful and lasting. Welcome to Jessica Alba's Honest Success: Building a Health and Wellness Empire.

Overview of Alba's Transition

Jessica Alba's journey from Hollywood starlet to a powerhouse founder of a billion-dollar company is nothing short of inspiring. Once known primarily for her roles in movies and TV, Alba transformed her career and public image by venturing into the world of health, wellness, and social impact. Her story is a testament to resilience, vision, and a strong sense of purpose. Through her transition, Alba not only redefined her career path but also built a brand that resonates with consumers seeking products that prioritize well-being and ethical responsibility.

After years in the entertainment industry, Alba grew increasingly concerned with the environmental impact of everyday products and the potential health risks they posed to families. This awareness sparked the creation of The Honest Company, a wellness and lifestyle brand dedicated to providing safe, sustainable, and transparent products for families. Alba saw an opportunity to fill a void in the market, recognizing that consumers were searching for safer and eco-friendly alternatives that aligned with their values.

The Honest Company embodies Alba's commitment to health and wellness through its emphasis on using natural, non-toxic ingredients. Alba's dedication to these values transformed her brand into more than just a business venture; it became a movement advocating for cleaner products and consumer transparency. Under her leadership, The Honest Company quickly evolved from a promising startup to a billion-dollar empire, setting a new standard in the industry and proving that socially conscious businesses can achieve remarkable financial success.

Alba's story touches on several key themes—health, wellness, and social impact—that are interwoven throughout her career shift. Her brand, The Honest Company, stands at the intersection of these themes, aiming to improve lives not only through the products themselves but also by raising awareness about the importance of sustainability and health-conscious choices. This transition has not only redefined Alba's professional identity but has also made her an influential figure in the growing field of social entrepreneurship.

Through her efforts, Alba has shown that pursuing purpose and profit need not be mutually exclusive. Her journey reminds readers that impactful change is possible, and that by prioritizing values, entrepreneurs can create lasting success that benefits both individuals and the planet.

Why She's Different:

Jessica Alba stands out as a true trailblazer, not just because of her star power but because of the unwavering authenticity, resilience, and commitment she brings to everything she does. While many actors have dipped their toes into business, few have built a legacy as impactful and innovative as Alba's. Her dedication to creating a brand that prioritizes health, safety, and environmental sustainability speaks volumes about her character, values, and vision for a healthier, more responsible world.

From the outset, Alba approached The Honest Company with a level of transparency and purpose that's rare in the industry. Her commitment to authenticity is evident not only in the brand's product lines but in her personal involvement, from development to marketing. Alba didn't just lend her name to the company; she built it from the ground up, deeply involved in the process of product research and testing. This hands-on approach made her brand unique, sending a clear message that she wasn't just another celebrity endorsement. Instead, she was an advocate for change, using her platform to bring attention to the hidden dangers in everyday household and personal care items.

In an industry where actors often face skepticism when entering business, Alba had to fight through numerous challenges and doubters. Early on, many questioned her dedication, dismissing her ambition as a fleeting celebrity project. But her resilience proved these critics wrong. Alba faced personal and professional setbacks, yet she never let them derail her mission. She persisted through the long, grueling hours, extensive product testing, and regulatory hurdles—all while balancing her roles as a mother, actress, and entrepreneur. Her resilience became the bedrock of The Honest Company, helping it evolve from a small startup to an industry-defining leader, valued in the billions and widely respected for its transparency and innovation.

Alba's unwavering commitment to creating safe, eco-friendly products has also set her apart in a marketplace saturated with companies that prioritize profit over safety. From day one, she insisted that her products be crafted without harmful chemicals, choosing natural, non-toxic ingredients wherever possible. This focus on safety was born from personal necessity; as a mother concerned about the chemicals her own children were exposed to, she was determined to find a better solution not just for her family but for families everywhere. Alba's commitment to eco-friendliness extends to her brand's packaging and manufacturing processes, which adhere to sustainable practices that minimize environmental impact, another rare priority in her industry.

In the face of so many challenges, Jessica Alba's unique blend of authenticity, resilience, and commitment to social responsibility has set her on a different path. Her success with The Honest Company is a testament to her authenticity as a founder and her willingness to remain true to her values, even in a market where taking shortcuts could have been the easier path. This dedication has earned her a loyal customer base and elevated her from Hollywood starlet to a respected leader in the world of social entrepreneurship. In an era where consumers are increasingly prioritizing integrity, transparency, and social impact, Alba's story resonates widely, proving that true authenticity and resilience can indeed change the world.

Chapter 1: From Silver Screen to Social Mission

Early Life and Hollywood Career

Jessica Alba's journey from humble beginnings to Hollywood stardom is marked by hard work, resilience, and an evolving personal mission that would later change her career—and the industry. Born in Pomona, California, Alba was raised in a modest, multicultural family that moved often due to her father's military career. Her childhood was also punctuated by serious health challenges, including frequent hospitalizations from illnesses like asthma, pneumonia, and severe allergies.

These early struggles had a profound impact on Alba, instilling in her a fierce determination to overcome obstacles and later inspiring her commitment to health-conscious living.

Alba's first taste of the entertainment world came early, as she began pursuing acting at age 12. Her big break arrived when she landed the lead role on the television series Dark Angel, created by acclaimed director James Cameron. Alba's portrayal of the genetically engineered super-soldier Max Guevera garnered widespread attention and critical acclaim, instantly establishing her as a new Hollywood starlet. Her career soared as she appeared in high-profile films, including Honey, Fantastic Four, Sin City, and Into the Blue. Known for her on-screen charm and versatility, Alba quickly became a favorite in both action roles and romantic comedies, showcasing her unique ability to captivate audiences across genres.

However, amid the glamour of Hollywood, Alba was quietly contending with an ongoing battle: her heightened sensitivity to chemicals and allergens. Even on set, she encountered reactions to makeup and skincare products, which often led to breakouts, respiratory issues, and other allergic responses. These experiences caused her to question the safety of the products she was using daily. As she researched, Alba was alarmed to discover that many personal care products contained harsh chemicals and additives linked to health risks. This newfound awareness planted the seeds of what would eventually become a personal mission to promote safe, clean alternatives—not only for herself but for others who faced similar issues.

Alba's dedication to clean, safe products became even more personal after she became a mother. Concerned about the products she would use on her children, Alba was increasingly frustrated by the lack of transparency in mainstream personal care items. She knew she wanted to raise her children in an environment free from toxic chemicals, but the options available on the market were limited and often costly. This frustration drove her to take matters into her own hands, embarking on a journey to create a brand that would provide safe, affordable, and effective products for families everywhere.

Alba's Hollywood success afforded her a platform and resources that she leveraged to make her vision a reality. Her background as a public figure helped bring attention to issues of chemical safety and eco-consciousness, sparking public conversations that were often ignored by the mainstream beauty and personal care industries. In many ways, her Hollywood career became the foundation of her next chapter as a wellness entrepreneur, providing her with both the credibility and the influence to make a significant impact.

Through The Honest Company, Alba was able to merge her passion for acting with a new, purpose-driven mission that would define the next phase of her life. Her early health struggles, coupled with her Hollywood career, laid the groundwork for her transition from actress to activist, and eventually, to a celebrated founder of a billion-dollar business focused on health, wellness, and transparency.

The Turning Point

The launch of The Honest Company was a pivotal moment for Jessica Alba, representing a bold departure from Hollywood glamour toward a mission-driven career in business. Alba's journey to founding a billion-dollar brand focused on health, safety, and eco-consciousness was anything but straightforward. In fact, it was marked by self-doubt, external skepticism, and a steep learning curve in an industry with little tolerance for "celebrity entrepreneurs." Yet it was precisely these challenges that ignited Alba's determination to succeed on her own terms, creating a brand that would resonate with countless families looking for safe, clean, and sustainable products.

Alba's transition from actress to entrepreneur began with a very personal need: her desire to protect her family from harmful chemicals and allergens. Frustrated by her own experiences with product sensitivities and the limited options for safe, accessible personal care products, she began conducting research into the ingredients and processes behind household items. Alba was stunned to find that many everyday products contained chemicals linked to various health risks. She felt a strong pull to do something about it, but she was uncertain about how to turn this passion into a viable business.

Around this time, Alba started sharing her findings with friends and family, who voiced similar frustrations and concerns about the lack of safe options. These conversations became a catalyst, convincing Alba that the need for transparent, clean products was not just her own; it was shared by parents and consumers everywhere. Armed with this knowledge, she began taking steps to turn her vision into reality, eventually conceptualizing The Honest Company as a brand dedicated to safety, transparency, and family-friendly values.

However, the path was far from easy. In an industry dominated by large corporations with vast resources, Alba faced immediate skepticism, especially due to her background as an actress. Many dismissed her entrepreneurial ambitions as a celebrity whim. Investors were reluctant, doubting that a Hollywood actress could navigate the complexities of business and questioning the longevity of her commitment. Alba found herself repeatedly defending her vision, having to convince skeptics that she was more than just a familiar face looking to cash in on her fame.

But Alba's resilience grew with each setback. She poured herself into understanding every detail of her business, from ingredient sourcing and product formulation to branding and regulatory compliance. Determined to prove her critics wrong, she assembled a team of industry experts who shared her commitment to safety and transparency. Alba was unafraid to ask questions, challenge assumptions, and even admit when she didn't know something—an approach that ultimately strengthened her leadership.

The roadblocks only fueled Alba's dedication, transforming her initial passion into an all-consuming mission. She began to understand that building The Honest Company wasn't just about creating a business; it was about proving that a consumer-first, health-conscious company could succeed in a market largely ruled by convenience and low-cost production. Alba's authenticity, coupled with her willingness to fight for her vision, set her apart from other celebrity entrepreneurs who often step back once their name is attached. Instead, Alba remained front and center, involved in every aspect of The Honest Company's operations,

Chapter 2: Crafting the Honest Brand

Brand Vision and Values: How Jessica conceptualized a company centered on transparency, integrity, and eco-friendly values.

Jessica Alba's vision for The Honest Company was born from a deeply personal desire to create a brand where health, safety, and transparency were paramount. Unlike many celebrity-led ventures, her mission wasn't driven by the appeal of profit or fame but by a genuine passion to solve a problem she and countless other parents faced: the need for safe, non-toxic products for their families. This sense of purpose became the foundation for the brand's core values, ultimately transforming The Honest

Company into a billion-dollar leader in the wellness industry.

Alba's journey to conceptualize a brand with integrity and transparency began with her early frustrations as a new mother. She had become increasingly aware of the lack of transparency in consumer products, particularly when it came to ingredients. Many baby and personal care products on the market contained chemicals with long, unpronounceable names, some of which were linked to harmful effects. Shocked by the lax regulatory standards that allowed such chemicals in everyday items, Alba saw a clear opportunity: to create a brand that put safety and integrity first.

The central pillar of Alba's vision was transparency, a quality she felt was largely absent in the industry. From her earliest conversations with prospective team members, Alba was adamant that The Honest Company would uphold a policy of complete openness. She wanted customers to know exactly what went into their products, with nothing hidden. This commitment to transparency extended beyond the products themselves and into Honest's communication practices, customer service, and marketing efforts. Alba ensured that everything about The Honest Company—from its sourcing practices to its environmental impact—was readily available to consumers, fostering a sense of trust and loyalty that few brands achieve.

Alba's dedication to eco-friendly values was also deeply personal, informed by her own concerns about the planet her children would inherit. From the start, she committed to using sustainable materials and practices throughout the company, understanding that eco-consciousness needed to be woven into every aspect of the business to have a meaningful impact. For example, The Honest Company's packaging uses recycled materials, and its manufacturing processes prioritize minimal waste and energy efficiency. Alba worked closely with suppliers who shared this vision, creating a supply chain that aligned with her environmental ideals. She made it a priority that every step—from sourcing raw ingredients to shipping products—would reflect the company's commitment to reducing its ecological footprint.

As the brand grew, Alba stayed true to her core value of integrity. She maintained a hands-on approach, carefully overseeing product development to ensure every item met the highest safety and quality standards. The Honest Company also implemented strict third-party testing and certifications, a practice that assured customers of the brand's commitment to safety and quality. Alba was determined to earn the trust of her customers not through flashy marketing or celebrity endorsements but through the consistent delivery of high-quality, trustworthy products. Her commitment to integrity also extended to Honest's social responsibility efforts, with a portion of the company's profits regularly directed toward charitable initiatives supporting families in need.

Beyond creating products, Alba wanted The Honest Company to serve as a catalyst for change in the industry. She actively campaigned for stricter regulations on ingredients used in personal care and household products, often partnering with advocacy groups to promote consumer safety and environmental protection. Through Honest, Alba envisioned a brand that not only provided safe alternatives but also inspired a broader movement toward transparency and ethical responsibility. She hoped to challenge other companies to prioritize people and the planet over profit, creating a ripple effect that would ultimately benefit both consumers and the environment.

Jessica Alba's vision for The Honest Company embodies her commitment to transparency, eco-friendly values, and unwavering integrity. She succeeded in building a brand that stands out in a crowded marketplace, offering products that align with the values of an increasingly informed and conscientious consumer base. The Honest

Company is more than a brand; it's a movement that reflects Alba's dedication to a healthier, more sustainable world, proving that business can thrive while putting values first. Through her vision and values, Alba has not only redefined her career but also set a new standard in the wellness and personal care industry.

Understanding the Market

Jessica Alba's journey to launch The Honest Company was underpinned by an intense period of market research and education. Unlike many celebrity-driven ventures that lean heavily on fame to promote products, Alba took a rigorous approach, diving deeply into understanding consumer needs and the complexities of sustainable production. Her dedication to creating a meaningful, value-driven brand led her to explore everything from market trends and consumer pain points to environmental challenges and supply chain logistics. Through this process, Alba gained a comprehensive understanding of the wellness and personal care industries, which empowered her to design a brand that truly addressed the needs of modern consumers while adhering to eco-friendly values.

When Alba first began contemplating the idea of creating her own company, she had a strong sense of what she wanted: safe, transparent, and environmentally conscious products. However, the specifics—how to create these products and how to make them affordable, accessible, and scalable—were entirely new territory for her. To bridge this gap, she embarked on a learning journey, consulting industry experts, reading extensively, and conducting her own informal surveys to gain insight into what consumers were looking for in personal care and household products. Alba sought to understand not only what people wanted but also the issues they faced with existing products on the market, particularly regarding ingredient safety, product efficacy, and transparency.

Alba's first major discovery was the lack of trust many consumers felt toward mainstream brands. She found that consumers were increasingly wary of products containing chemicals and additives they couldn't understand or trust. Parents, in particular, expressed frustration at the lack of safe options for children. Driven by these insights, Alba committed to creating a company that would prioritize transparency above all else. She wanted to ensure that Honest's products would list every ingredient in plain language, empowering consumers to make informed choices.

Her commitment to eco-friendly, sustainable production was equally shaped by her research. Alba learned that many consumers were seeking brands that not only provided safe products but also minimized their environmental impact. Recognizing the growing demand for eco-conscious brands, Alba made sustainable production a core tenet of The Honest Company. She researched sustainable materials, ethical sourcing practices, and energy-efficient manufacturing processes, ultimately partnering with suppliers and manufacturers who aligned with these values. Alba was also determined to address the waste associated with packaging, opting for recyclable materials whenever possible to reduce the environmental footprint of each product.

Through her research, Alba also learned that affordability was a crucial factor for many consumers, particularly parents. She understood that while people were willing to pay a premium for quality, many families could not afford the high costs often associated with "clean" and "green" products. Alba made it a priority to find ways to keep The Honest Company's products affordable without compromising on quality. This commitment led her to work closely with her supply chain partners to optimize costs and find efficiencies, ensuring her products could reach a wide audience without sacrificing her brand's values.

Alba's journey to understand the market also extended to learning about the complexities of ingredient safety and regulation. She quickly realized that the standards for personal care products were surprisingly lax, with many potentially harmful chemicals still in use. This discovery fueled her desire to create products that were not only effective but also genuinely safe for long-term use. Alba consulted toxicologists, chemists, and other industry professionals to understand the potential health impacts of various ingredients. She established strict internal standards for The Honest Company, going beyond the minimum legal requirements to ensure that each product met the highest standards of safety.

Throughout her research, Alba remained committed to listening to consumers. She attended industry events, spoke directly with families, and engaged with parents and caregivers to gather firsthand feedback. This focus on customer insights allowed her to refine Honest's offerings continuously, ensuring that each product would meet the evolving needs and expectations of her target audience. Alba's willingness to learn and adapt was key to shaping a brand that resonated deeply with consumers who were increasingly seeking products aligned with their values.

In understanding the market, Alba not only identified a gap but also gained the knowledge to fill it effectively. Her journey was a transformative experience that underscored her belief that businesses could be both profitable and purpose-driven. By combining insights into consumer needs with a dedication to sustainable production, Alba crafted a brand that addressed real issues faced by everyday people while championing ethical practices in an industry often criticized for prioritizing profit over people and the planet. This commitment to truly understanding her market set The Honest Company apart, enabling it to become a trusted name for families looking for safe, transparent, and eco-conscious choices.

Chapter 3: Building from Scratch

Funding and Finding Partners: Her challenges in securing funding and her search for partners who believed in her mission.

Securing funding and finding the right partners were two of the most challenging yet crucial steps in Jessica Alba's journey to launch The Honest Company. Transitioning from Hollywood into the world of business, Alba was well aware of the skepticism she might face as a "celebrity entrepreneur" entering a competitive, established industry. Despite her passion and clear vision, securing initial funding for The Honest Company proved far more difficult than she had anticipated. Investors were cautious, doubting whether an actress could successfully launch and sustain a brand in the competitive sectors of wellness and personal care. However, Alba's relentless pursuit of her mission, coupled with her unique approach, eventually won over the partners who would help bring her vision to life.

Early in her journey, Alba faced significant hurdles in getting potential investors to take her seriously. Many were reluctant to invest in a business led by someone outside the industry, especially one with no formal business background. For them, Alba's Hollywood fame was more a liability than an asset, raising concerns that she might not have the skills or knowledge to succeed as a founder. Moreover, the concept of a clean, eco-friendly product line—especially one that was transparent and free of potentially harmful chemicals—was still emerging at the time, making investors wary about the long-term viability of the business.

But Alba was undeterred by these doubts. Driven by her mission, she committed herself to learning every aspect of the industry and educating investors on the growing demand for safe, sustainable products. Alba wasn't just looking for funding; she was searching for partners who believed in her values and were genuinely aligned with her mission. She knew that the right partners could make a tremendous difference, not only financially but also in terms of experience, support, and shared passion.

In her search for allies, Alba found a key supporter in Brian Lee, a serial entrepreneur known for founding companies like LegalZoom and ShoeDazzle. Lee was initially skeptical of the idea, but Alba's genuine passion for creating a healthier, safer world for families won him over. Lee recognized the authenticity in her mission and saw potential in her vision, leading him to become not only an investor but also a co-founder. With his experience and guidance, he played a pivotal role in helping Alba navigate the complexities of business operations and product development. Together, they began to build the framework for The Honest Company, grounded in the shared values of transparency, safety, and eco-consciousness.

Another major step in finding the right partners involved assembling a team that could bring her vision to life. Alba sought out experts with a track record in consumer goods, health, and safety to ensure that The Honest Company would be built on a foundation of scientific rigor and ethical practices. She worked to recruit individuals who believed in the brand's mission just as much as she did, creating a team that was not only skilled but also dedicated to the brand's purpose. Her early hires included product developers and chemists who shared her commitment to safety and transparency, and they were instrumental in developing formulas that met her strict safety standards.

Alba's determination ultimately attracted investors who recognized the untapped potential of the wellness market and the growing demand for clean, safe products. By demonstrating both her commitment and her knowledge, she was able to secure early investments that allowed The Honest Company to scale production, develop an online platform, and build a strong, recognizable brand presence. These initial funds helped the company make its mark, launching a line of products that resonated deeply with a new generation of health-conscious consumers.

Yet Alba's quest for partners didn't stop there; she continued to seek out and align herself with people and organizations that shared her commitment to creating positive change. The Honest Company eventually attracted major investors, including L Catterton and Institutional Venture Partners, who brought the resources and expertise needed to expand the brand further. These partnerships allowed The Honest Company to accelerate its growth, enter retail spaces, and diversify its product offerings, all while maintaining the commitment to transparency and safety that Alba had set from the start.

Jessica Alba's journey to secure funding and find the right partners reflects her resilience, passion, and commitment to her mission. In the face of skepticism and obstacles, she never compromised on her values, insisting on finding partners who believed not only in her potential as a business leader but also in the greater purpose of The Honest Company. Through her dedication and unyielding vision, Alba succeeded in building a business that went beyond products to create a meaningful impact, proving that with the right partners and a clear mission, it is possible to change the industry for the better.

Learning Business Basics: How she navigated the shift from entertainment to business and built a team that aligned with her values.

Jessica Alba's transition from the world of entertainment to business was a bold and challenging journey. Despite her considerable fame as a Hollywood actress, she was venturing into entirely new territory when she founded The Honest Company. Alba quickly realized that, while her vision was clear, the skills required to build a successful business were complex and multifaceted. Determined to succeed and make a difference, she immersed herself in learning business fundamentals, from operational logistics to financial management, and surrounded herself with experts who could bring her vision to life. Her willingness to step into a role as a learner—not just a leader—allowed her to build a brand rooted in her values of transparency, safety, and sustainability, while also mastering the practicalities of running a company.

One of Alba's first steps was to acknowledge the skills she didn't yet possess and seek guidance from those who had experience in the business world. She understood that her celebrity status alone wouldn't be enough to guarantee success. The consumer goods and wellness industries were crowded, competitive, and filled with seasoned professionals. Alba knew that her company would need to stand out on more than just her name; it would have to be credible, authentic, and, above all, effective in delivering on its promises. To this end, she sought mentors and advisors from diverse fields who could help her develop her business acumen and navigate the intricacies of building a successful company from scratch.

One of Alba's most important decisions was to partner with Brian Lee, a seasoned entrepreneur known for co-founding successful companies like LegalZoom and ShoeDazzle. Lee not only provided crucial mentorship but also helped Alba understand the basics of business structure, legal considerations, and the challenges of scaling a brand. With his guidance, Alba gained insight into the operational and strategic aspects of business, such as supply chain management, pricing, and market positioning. Lee's experience helped Alba learn how to avoid common pitfalls that many new businesses face and provided her with a framework for making smart, sustainable decisions.

Learning business basics also meant Alba had to embrace the complexities of financial management—an area that was entirely new to her. She recognized the importance of understanding cash flow, profit margins, and budgeting, which would ultimately be essential for The Honest Company's long-term sustainability. Alba worked closely with financial advisors to grasp the financial metrics that would drive the business forward and learned how to make sound, data-driven decisions. Her commitment to learning extended to understanding funding cycles, investor expectations, and the nuances of budgeting effectively to sustain the company's growth. In doing so, Alba transformed her understanding of money from a personal perspective to one that was strategic and essential for the brand's success.

Building a strong team that shared her commitment to safe, eco-friendly products was another critical piece of the puzzle. Alba knew she needed to bring together individuals with expertise in product development, environmental safety, consumer research, and marketing—areas where she lacked direct experience. She was selective in her hiring, choosing people who not only had strong skills but also shared her values and passion for creating change in the wellness industry. By assembling a team aligned with her mission, Alba ensured that everyone working on The Honest Company felt invested in the purpose and potential of the brand.

In product development, for example, Alba worked with experts who specialized in non-toxic ingredients and sustainable practices. Together, they created a process for evaluating every ingredient, ensuring that Honest products met high safety standards while being environmentally friendly. Alba was hands-on in this phase, involved in everything from product testing to packaging design. Her attention to detail in product development demonstrated her commitment to learning and her determination to create products that she would feel comfortable using for her own family. This authenticity became a core value of The Honest Company, and it helped the brand gain credibility and trust with consumers.

Alba also immersed herself in understanding customer insights and consumer psychology, learning about the factors that influenced purchasing decisions in her target market. She recognized that creating a brand that resonated with families required empathy and a deep understanding of their everyday needs and concerns. Alba's openness to feedback and her willingness to listen to parents, caregivers, and eco-conscious consumers allowed her to make informed decisions that kept the brand in tune with its audience. She paid close attention to customer reviews, conducted surveys, and held focus groups to gather real-time insights. This hands-on approach helped her refine Honest's product line and ensured that it remained relevant and responsive to consumer demands.

Another key area of learning for Alba was brand management and marketing. She quickly discovered that building brand awareness would require a strategic and nuanced approach, particularly as she wanted to avoid the typical "celebrity brand" label. Alba collaborated with her marketing team to develop an identity for The Honest Company that was genuine and relatable. She prioritized transparency in all communications, including clear labeling on packaging and open discussions about product ingredients. This transparency became a cornerstone of the brand's reputation and helped set it apart in a crowded market where trust was often lacking.

Through her journey of learning business fundamentals, Alba transformed herself from an actress and advocate into a knowledgeable and strategic CEO. Her determination to understand every aspect of the business enabled her to make decisions that stayed true to her values and her mission of creating a safer, healthier world for families. By mastering the basics and building a team aligned with her vision, Alba successfully navigated the shift from entertainment to business, ultimately building a billion-dollar brand that has redefined consumer expectations in the wellness industry. Her story underscores the power of resilience, authenticity, and a commitment to continuous learning—qualities that have made The Honest Company a trusted leader in the world of clean, sustainable products.

Chapter 4: Breaking Through Stereotypes

The "Celebrity Brand" Dilemma: Overcoming initial criticisms and breaking down how she handled perceptions around celebrity businesses.

Launching The Honest Company, Jessica Alba faced one of the most persistent obstacles any celebrity entrepreneur encounters: the "celebrity brand" label. In a marketplace already crowded with famous faces backing products, Alba knew that her genuine commitment to safer, eco-friendly products might be overshadowed by the skepticism often aimed at celebrity ventures. Many high-profile brands launched by actors, athletes, and musicians fail to resonate because they come across as short-lived trends or publicity stunts rather than real commitments. Alba's challenge, then, was not only to build a successful company but to prove to both consumers and the industry that The Honest Company was driven by passion and authenticity, not just a recognizable name.

From the outset, Alba was acutely aware of the "celebrity brand" dilemma. She understood that in many people's eyes, her transition from actress to entrepreneur could seem superficial, like an attempt to leverage her fame for financial gain. Moreover, the wellness and personal care sectors are already competitive and specialized; a celebrity entering this space could be seen as out of touch or lacking expertise. Many wondered if Alba would truly be involved in the day-to-day running of the business, or if her name was simply a logo on a bottle. The unspoken question hanging over The Honest Company was: "Is this brand really different, or is it just another celebrity product?"

However, Alba's approach was entirely different. She began her journey into the business not from a desire to expand her career but from a personal mission to solve a problem that she believed was crucial for families everywhere. Alba's own health challenges and experiences as a mother had sparked a real, urgent interest in safer products for children and families. She knew firsthand the struggles parents faced in finding products that were genuinely safe, clean, and environmentally friendly, and she became determined to build a company that provided exactly that. Alba believed that her purpose-driven mission would help dispel the image of The Honest Company as merely a "celebrity brand."

One of Alba's first steps in overcoming the "celebrity brand" stigma was to commit herself fully to learning the business. She wasn't interested in being the face of a brand she didn't fully understand or care about; she wanted to lead from the front. She immersed herself in research, learning the ins and outs of the personal care and wellness industry, from ingredient sourcing to manufacturing processes. Alba's willingness to become a student of the business showed investors, industry professionals, and eventually consumers that she was serious about creating change. By rolling up her sleeves and building expertise in product safety, eco-friendly packaging, and consumer health, Alba demonstrated that The Honest Company was about more than her name—it was about her mission.

Transparency was another essential strategy Alba used to combat the "celebrity brand" dilemma. She insisted on full transparency not only in the ingredients used in Honest products but also in the company's values and business practices. Unlike many celebrity brands that leverage the allure of luxury, secrecy, or exclusivity, The Honest Company took a radically open approach, providing customers with clear and accessible information about what went into each product and why. The company's commitment to transparency became one of its most defining characteristics and helped set it apart in an industry where hidden chemicals and vague labels are often the norm. Alba wanted consumers to feel they could trust Honest's products for their own families, and her insistence on transparency built credibility and trust.

Another key part of her approach was the careful selection of her team and partners. Alba didn't rely on Hollywood agents or industry connections to assemble her team; instead, she sought out experts in health, safety, product development, and environmental science. Her team included professionals with decades of experience who shared her commitment to clean, ethical products and were just as passionate about redefining industry standards. These partnerships were strategic and deliberate, helping to cement Honest's reputation as a serious, credible brand. By surrounding herself with industry veterans and professionals who believed in her mission, Alba was able to show that The Honest Company was far more than just her name and face—it was built on a solid foundation of knowledge, expertise, and shared values.

Alba also took a different approach to marketing and branding. Rather than relying on her celebrity status to promote the brand, she positioned herself as a founder and CEO who understood her products on a personal level. When she appeared in marketing materials, she did so not as a glamorous actress but as a mother and advocate, sharing her journey and values directly with consumers. In interviews, she openly discussed her personal motivations and the health issues that inspired her commitment to safer products, underscoring her authenticity and relatability. This approach resonated with a wide audience, particularly families, who saw Alba as a parent advocating for the same values they held. By focusing on shared values rather than on celebrity appeal, Alba was able to create a brand that connected with people on a deeply personal level.

Her strategy paid off. Instead of being dismissed as just another celebrity brand, The Honest Company rapidly gained traction as a trusted name in wellness, baby care, and personal care products. Consumers responded positively to Honest's transparency and Alba's commitment, and industry insiders began to recognize that she was serious about changing the sector. The company quickly became known for its rigorous product safety standards and dedication to environmental sustainability, further distancing itself from the superficiality often associated with celebrity ventures.

Alba's persistence in proving herself and her brand's values won over skeptics, shifting the narrative around Honest from a "celebrity business" to a genuinely impactful, mission-driven company.

The Honest Company's success has become a model for how celebrities can transition into entrepreneurship without relying solely on their fame. Alba's story showcases the importance of authenticity, hard work, and a true commitment to one's values in building a meaningful brand. By facing the "celebrity brand" dilemma head-on, Jessica Alba transformed Honest into a billion-dollar business that is respected not only for its products but also for the integrity and purpose behind them. Her journey demonstrates that with the right approach, a brand can transcend its celebrity origins and become a force for positive change.

Proving Herself: Stories of her involvement in product development, branding, and public perception.

Jessica Alba knew that transforming The Honest Company from a concept into a billion-dollar brand would require much more than her celebrity name. To succeed in an industry filled with well-established players and high consumer expectations, she needed to prove herself as more than just a Hollywood figure dabbling in business. She had to be the driving force behind every detail, from product development to branding and managing public perception. This meant getting deeply involved in each step of the process, showing not just investors and industry peers, but also consumers, that she was committed to her mission. Her active role in shaping the company's products, image, and reputation was crucial in establishing Honest as a trusted, pioneering brand in the wellness and eco-friendly market.

One of the most telling stories of Alba's involvement was in the area of product development—a realm that is notoriously complex and requires a deep understanding of science, safety, and compliance. Alba had a personal stake in every product that The Honest Company released, driven by her own health concerns and her experience as a mother. She didn't simply sign off on ingredients or formulas; instead, she immersed herself in the research and development process. Alba insisted on understanding each ingredient and its potential impact, often sitting in on meetings with scientists, chemists, and environmental experts to learn the risks and benefits of every component. She was known to ask questions until she fully understood the implications of product decisions, ensuring that they aligned with her vision of non-toxic, family-friendly products. This level of dedication was unusual for celebrity founders and demonstrated her commitment to making Honest products as safe and effective as possible.

Alba's hands-on approach extended to the testing and refinement phases of product development. She actively participated in early product trials, using her own family as the first testers. Whether it was baby wipes, personal care items, or cleaning products, Alba made sure that she and her children tested everything personally. She paid attention to every detail: scent, texture, packaging, and effectiveness. If something didn't meet her high standards, she pushed for improvements, even if it meant extending the production timeline. Alba once recounted how she went back and forth with her team for months on a diaper design, tweaking the materials and structure until she was confident it would work for parents and babies alike. By being so involved, Alba was able to directly influence the quality of Honest products, reinforcing her commitment to creating items she could genuinely stand behind.

When it came to branding, Alba's influence was equally significant. She recognized early on that Honest's success would depend on its ability to differentiate itself as a brand with purpose and integrity. To achieve this, she was deeply involved in shaping Honest's brand identity, ensuring it reflected her own values and the mission she set out to accomplish. Alba wanted the branding to communicate the company's commitment to transparency, safety, and eco-consciousness, so she collaborated closely with marketing and design teams to create a visual identity that conveyed simplicity, cleanliness, and trustworthiness. She had a strong opinion on color schemes, logo designs, and packaging that felt approachable yet sophisticated, and she often gave feedback on how to improve each aspect to align better with Honest's values.

One of her key branding initiatives was Honest's transparent communication with consumers. She insisted that the company be upfront about ingredients and production processes, setting it apart from competitors who often masked their products behind vague labels and hidden chemicals. Alba championed a "radical transparency" approach, where every ingredient and process was disclosed, even if it revealed the challenges Honest faced in achieving completely natural products. By allowing consumers to understand the ingredients and methods behind each product, Alba fostered a sense of trust and openness that was rare in the industry. She knew this honesty would resonate, especially with parents and health-conscious consumers who valued full disclosure and wanted to make informed choices.

Managing public perception was another area where Alba's direct involvement proved invaluable. Alba was acutely aware that public skepticism of "celebrity brands" was widespread, and she wanted to demonstrate that her commitment was genuine and enduring. She frequently participated in interviews, media appearances, and speaking engagements where she shared her personal story and the motivations behind Honest's founding. Alba was open about the health issues she'd experienced growing up, her fears as a new mom, and her genuine passion for creating safer products for other families. By telling her story authentically, she helped the public see that Honest was not just another celebrity vanity project but a mission-driven company created out of a desire for real change.

Alba also tackled criticism head-on, particularly when Honest faced public scrutiny over product recalls and ingredient controversies. She didn't hide from these issues but addressed them directly, taking responsibility and communicating Honest's efforts to improve. For example, when the company faced backlash over a sunscreen that some customers said was ineffective, Alba took it seriously. She issued a public statement, apologized, and directed her team to review and improve the product. Rather than deflecting blame, Alba used the incident as an opportunity to reinforce Honest's commitment to quality and consumer trust, promising greater testing and transparency moving forward. By addressing concerns openly, she turned a potential setback into an opportunity to strengthen the brand's values and reassure its audience.

Alba's investment in Honest's success went beyond the typical role of a founder; she was deeply embedded in the company's culture and operations. She regularly spent time with different teams—whether in product development, marketing, or customer service—offering insights, support, and a clear vision of what Honest should stand for. This hands-on involvement created a culture where employees felt motivated and connected to the brand's mission, knowing that their founder was as dedicated as they were to making a difference. Alba's authenticity and willingness to learn also inspired her team, as they saw her actively learning, adjusting, and pushing for improvements based on feedback. Her presence and influence were felt across the company, shaping it from the inside out.

Through her hands-on involvement, Alba demonstrated that The Honest Company was not merely a business venture but a personal mission she was fully committed to achieving. By proving herself at every stage of the process, she transformed Honest from a "celebrity brand" into a reputable and respected player in the wellness industry. Her dedication to product quality, brand integrity, and public accountability established her as a credible entrepreneur and an advocate for change in an industry that had long prioritized profits over safety. Alba's journey illustrates that true dedication and authenticity can overcome public skepticism, and that a hands-on approach can be the key to building a brand that endures.

Chapter 5: Navigating the Challenges of Growth

Product Challenges and Launch: From prototyping to quality control, Alba's hands-on approach to bringing products to market.

For Jessica Alba, the journey to launching The Honest Company's first product line was a rigorous, hands-on process filled with challenges that demanded her personal attention to detail, determination, and resilience. Unlike many celebrity ventures where the founder lends only a name, Alba was immersed in each phase of product development, from initial prototyping to navigating quality control obstacles. Her vision for Honest was clear from the start: to create safe, eco-friendly products that parents could trust. This commitment to quality and safety meant that Alba would accept nothing less than the highest standards, even if it meant delaying launch dates or investing more time and resources into refining products.

One of Alba's first hurdles was establishing a clear, stringent set of guidelines for Honest products. From the outset, she was adamant that every item bearing the

Honest name would avoid common chemicals found in mainstream consumer products, such as parabens, sulfates, and synthetic fragrances. However, developing effective alternatives without these ingredients was no small feat. Alba quickly discovered that the market for non-toxic, eco-friendly ingredients was still relatively limited, meaning her team would need to pioneer new formulas and production methods. This led to months of experimentation, testing, and failures. Alba worked closely with chemists, environmental scientists, and product engineers, actively participating in product trials and sitting in on laboratory meetings to understand the challenges her team faced. Her hands-on involvement allowed her to make informed decisions on which ingredients to include and which compromises, if any, could be made in the final products.

One of the early products that presented a major challenge was the diaper—an essential item in Honest's lineup that had to be hypoallergenic, durable, and affordable. Alba knew that many traditional diapers contained harsh chemicals and weren't biodegradable, so she was determined to create an option that prioritized safety and environmental responsibility. However, making a diaper that was both effective and eco-friendly proved to be a substantial challenge. She pushed her team to consider different materials and conduct durability tests, often going through numerous prototypes before landing on a design she felt confident in. Alba even used her own children to test early versions, closely observing factors like absorption, comfort, and potential skin reactions. After months of trial and error, Honest finally developed a diaper that met her rigorous standards for both safety and performance. This meticulous, hands-on process demonstrated Alba's deep investment in Honest's values, showing consumers that she was committed to delivering truly high-quality products.

Quality control was another area where Alba's involvement was instrumental. She understood that quality control wasn't just a final step in production but an ongoing commitment to maintaining Honest's reputation and consumer trust. To ensure that each product met the company's standards, Alba insisted on regular checks throughout the development process. She established partnerships with third-party testing labs that specialized in eco-friendly and non-toxic certifications. Alba wanted Honest's products to not only meet internal standards but also gain independent verification from reputable organizations in the industry. By going above and beyond in quality control measures, Alba set Honest apart as a brand that consumers could trust.

The path to launching Honest's first product line was anything but smooth. As Honest neared the launch phase,

Alba encountered logistical hurdles that would test her perseverance and adaptability. Sourcing eco-friendly materials at a large scale proved challenging, as few suppliers were equipped to meet Honest's demand without compromising on sustainability. Alba was directly involved in finding and vetting suppliers, often visiting manufacturing sites to ensure that each partner aligned with Honest's ethical and environmental standards. This personal engagement allowed her to build relationships with suppliers who understood and supported her mission, a crucial step in establishing a supply chain that could scale while remaining true to Honest's values.

Alba's dedication to overseeing every detail also extended to packaging—a component of the product experience that she viewed as an extension of Honest's brand identity. She was insistent that packaging be both aesthetically pleasing and environmentally responsible. Alba sat in on design meetings, choosing natural colors and minimalistic designs that reflected the simplicity and purity of the products within. She also worked with packaging engineers to select recyclable or compostable materials wherever possible, ensuring that Honest's commitment to sustainability was evident in every aspect of the product. The end result was packaging that communicated Honest's values and differentiated it on store shelves, drawing consumers who prioritized eco-friendly brands.

Perhaps one of the most formidable challenges Alba faced was skepticism from potential retail partners and investors, who questioned whether consumers would buy into a brand with a strong eco-friendly focus and a commitment to transparency. Many established companies were accustomed to maximizing profits by cutting corners on ingredients and production costs, and they doubted that Honest's approach would be sustainable or commercially viable. Alba's response was to double down on her mission, taking every opportunity to educate retailers and investors on the growing demand for safe, clean products. She met with numerous stakeholders to discuss Honest's goals and provided them with detailed market research that showcased consumer trends toward healthier, environmentally friendly options. Her persistence paid off, as she ultimately secured key partnerships that helped launch Honest's products in major retail chains.

Finally, Alba took an active role in the marketing strategy for Honest's initial product launch. She recognized that the public needed to understand what made Honest different from other brands, so she invested in educating consumers about the ingredients and production values behind each product. Alba personally engaged with media outlets, bloggers, and influencers, sharing her story and Honest's mission in a way that was relatable and inspiring.

Her visibility in the media helped bring credibility to the brand, as consumers saw a founder who was passionate and deeply knowledgeable about the products. Honest's launch was supported by Alba's authenticity and hands-on approach, resonating with a growing audience of health-conscious, eco-minded consumers who were seeking trustworthy brands.

Ultimately, Alba's hands-on involvement in each phase of product development, from prototyping to quality control, was instrumental in shaping Honest's success. Her commitment to authenticity, safety, and sustainability permeated every aspect of the company, proving that she was more than a celebrity face. By actively engaging in the hard work and problem-solving needed to bring Honest's products to market, she showed that she was a founder determined to make a real impact. Her dedication to quality, transparency, and consumer trust not only set Honest apart but also set a new standard for celebrity entrepreneurs and eco-conscious brands alike.

Facing Setbacks: Navigating challenges like product recalls, legal issues, and public scrutiny with transparency.

As The Honest Company gained traction in the marketplace, Jessica Alba quickly learned that success in business came with its own set of formidable challenges.

From product recalls to legal issues and intense public scrutiny, Alba faced numerous obstacles that tested her resolve and the resilience of her company's values. Unlike some entrepreneurs who might sidestep or downplay problems, Alba believed in addressing these issues directly and with full transparency—a principle she felt was critical to maintaining consumer trust and the ethical standards she had built her brand around. Her approach to setbacks not only underscored her commitment to honesty but also set a new precedent in how companies, especially those led by public figures, handle adversity in the public eye.

One of the most significant challenges Alba encountered was product recalls—a sensitive issue for any consumer goods company, but especially for a brand like Honest that built its identity on safety and reliability. Alba was well aware of the reputational risk that recalls posed, particularly for a company with such a deeply personal connection to its founder. However, when faced with quality concerns, she chose to handle recalls head-on rather than risk compromising the trust she had established with her consumers. Early in Honest's growth, the company faced scrutiny over issues with its sunscreen product, which some customers claimed was ineffective. Photos and stories circulated across social media, showing sunburns that consumers attributed to Honest's sunscreen, creating a public relations storm that put Honest's safety-first mission under a microscope.

Instead of evading the issue, Alba and her team addressed the complaints directly. Honest conducted an internal review, communicated openly with customers, and ultimately issued a response that reaffirmed their commitment to quality and consumer safety. Alba personally took part in addressing concerns, making sure that the public understood Honest's intentions and steps to prevent future issues. She recognized that simply issuing a recall or removing the product from shelves would not be enough to reassure customers—she needed to demonstrate that Honest was willing to learn from its mistakes. Her transparency in acknowledging the sunscreen issue helped restore some consumer faith, showing that Honest was a company that listened and was responsive to its community. By treating setbacks as learning opportunities, Alba managed to transform a potentially damaging event into a moment of growth for Honest, refining internal processes and quality standards as a result.

Legal challenges also tested Alba's commitment to transparency and her ability to manage high-stakes, high-pressure situations. As Honest grew, so did the scrutiny over its marketing claims and ingredient lists. In an industry with varied definitions of terms like "natural" and "non-toxic," Honest faced lawsuits alleging that certain products did not fully align with the company's advertised claims. These lawsuits posed a threat not only to Honest's reputation but also to its core values, as Alba was adamant about keeping the brand free of harmful chemicals and committed to providing safe alternatives. She worked closely with her legal team to address the accusations, but she also took it upon herself to clarify the company's position publicly, reaffirming her dedication to transparency. Honest adjusted its labeling practices to provide even clearer information for consumers, showing that the brand was responsive and dedicated to maintaining trust.

Public scrutiny over Honest's eco-friendly and non-toxic claims brought intense media attention, with some critics accusing Alba of greenwashing—a term used for companies that overstate their environmental efforts. For Honest, a brand built on authenticity, these accusations struck at the heart of its identity, and Alba took them very seriously. She responded by doubling down on her mission to be transparent, initiating third-party testing and certifications for Honest products to verify their claims. By doing so, she aimed to demonstrate that Honest wasn't merely marketing itself as eco-friendly but was genuinely committed to sustainable practices. The decision to engage with independent certifiers not only validated Honest's product claims but also served as a powerful statement of Alba's dedication to walking the talk.

Chapter 6: Scaling with a Purpose

Expansion and Product Diversification: How Alba and her team scaled Honest Co., launching skincare, baby care, and beauty products.

As The Honest Company established itself in the marketplace, Jessica Alba and her team recognized an exciting opportunity to expand beyond their initial product lines and diversify into new categories that aligned with Honest's mission. Starting with core baby products like diapers and wipes, the company gradually grew to offer a range of products that spanned skincare, baby care, and eventually beauty, each reflecting Honest's values of safety, sustainability, and transparency. This expansion into new categories was both a strategic business decision and a natural extension of Alba's original vision to provide families with high-quality, non-toxic options in every aspect of their lives.

For Alba, the path to product diversification was driven by a deep commitment to her consumers, many of whom had become loyal advocates of the Honest brand. She saw firsthand how customers were using Honest products as integral parts of their lives, and this community-inspired approach fueled her motivation to offer a more comprehensive suite of items. Alba listened closely to consumer feedback, often engaging with Honest's online communities, reading customer reviews, and even visiting stores to understand firsthand what people wanted from the brand. This active engagement provided valuable insights, revealing demand for a broader array of clean products—from skincare essentials for the whole family to beauty items that could redefine industry standards. Alba's personal investment in connecting with her customer base allowed Honest to tailor its expansion with precision, ensuring that every new product category met an existing need or desire within the Honest community.

The expansion into skincare was one of Honest's earliest steps toward broadening its product line. Alba saw the importance of offering skincare solutions that were free of harsh chemicals, sulfates, and artificial fragrances. She worked with her product development team to create a line that would appeal to individuals and families looking for effective, gentle, and safe skincare options. Products like gentle cleansers, lotions, and sunscreens were formulated with Honest's signature "no compromise" approach, using plant-based ingredients and sustainable sourcing practices wherever possible. Alba was deeply involved in the R&D phase, personally testing formulations and providing feedback on product feel, scent, and efficacy. Her attention to detail ensured that Honest's skincare line resonated with consumers who trusted the brand's dedication to safety. The launch was successful, strengthening Honest's position as a go-to brand for conscious consumers and helping the company establish a foothold in the competitive skincare market.

Building on the success of Honest's skincare products, Alba and her team next turned their focus to expanding the baby care line—a natural choice, given Honest's origins and core customer base of young families. While Honest had initially launched with diapers and wipes, Alba wanted to go further, envisioning a holistic line that included gentle shampoos, conditioners, body washes, and balms specifically formulated for babies' delicate skin. She understood that parents were often cautious about what they used on their children, especially newborns, and she was determined to create a baby care line that would set a new standard for safety. Alba's dedication to quality and her insistence on rigorous safety testing became key selling points, reassuring parents that Honest's baby products could be trusted with their children's health. The expanded baby care line became a cornerstone of Honest's identity, solidifying its reputation as a family-friendly brand that prioritized health, safety, and simplicity.

In a bold move to broaden Honest's reach, Alba and her team ventured into beauty, an industry historically known for synthetic ingredients and limited transparency around product formulations. This new line, Honest Beauty, was a significant step in Honest's growth, as it entered a crowded and competitive market with established giants. Yet Alba was confident that Honest could stand out by adhering to the values that had made it successful in other categories: clean ingredients, transparency, and a commitment to quality. She wanted to create beauty products that were safe, non-toxic, and inclusive, appealing to consumers looking for makeup and skincare that aligned with their health and ethical priorities.

The Honest Beauty line launched with an array of products, including foundation, mascara, lipstick, and skincare staples, each developed with plant-based ingredients and eco-conscious packaging. Alba played a crucial role in branding and positioning Honest Beauty, engaging in product testing, approving packaging designs, and even featuring in marketing campaigns to highlight the products' safe and effective qualities. She wanted consumers to see that Honest Beauty was an extension of the values they trusted from the core Honest brand, making beauty products accessible to those who might have avoided conventional cosmetics due to concerns about toxic chemicals. Alba's active role and personal endorsement of Honest Beauty helped build credibility, distinguishing the line as a genuinely clean beauty option rather than a typical celebrity-backed venture.

The expansion into these new categories came with significant operational challenges that Alba and her team had to navigate. As Honest grew, scaling production while maintaining quality and consistency became a priority. Alba insisted on partnering with manufacturers who understood Honest's mission and could adhere to its strict quality standards, visiting facilities and working closely with the operations team to ensure that growth did not compromise Honest's values. In addition, Alba and her team invested in expanding the company's supply chain and distribution networks, allowing Honest products to reach a wider audience both online and in major retail stores. This growth required Alba to deepen her understanding of logistics and distribution, areas where she had little experience at the start. Her willingness to learn, combined with her insistence on upholding Honest's principles, played a key role in building a robust operational foundation for Honest's continued expansion.

Throughout this period of growth, Alba remained mindful of Honest's brand identity and mission, ensuring that new product launches stayed true to the company's commitment to safe, eco-friendly, and accessible options. Her hands-on approach and dedication to quality fostered a culture within Honest that prioritized consumer trust and environmental responsibility. The brand's diversified portfolio allowed Honest to meet a range of consumer needs, positioning it as a lifestyle brand that offered clean, sustainable options across multiple facets of daily life.

Ultimately, Honest's expansion and product diversification were more than just business decisions—they were extensions of Alba's personal mission to create a safer world for her family and other families like hers. By launching skincare, baby care, and beauty products, Alba positioned Honest as a comprehensive solution for health-conscious consumers. Her hands-on leadership, consumer-centric approach, and unwavering commitment to the brand's values were instrumental in Honest's growth, proving that it was possible to scale while staying true to a mission of integrity and transparency.

Maintaining Brand Integrity: Ensuring the company's mission and values remain intact amid rapid growth and scaling.

As The Honest Company scaled from a small startup to a powerhouse in the consumer goods industry, Jessica Alba faced the critical challenge of preserving the brand's core mission and values amid rapid growth. In an industry where expansion often comes at the expense of original principles, Alba knew that keeping Honest's mission intact would require careful planning, a commitment to transparency, and strategic decision-making at every stage of growth. Honest's brand identity was built on ideals like safety, sustainability, and trust, and Alba was determined to maintain these values no matter how much the company expanded. This dedication to brand integrity became one of the company's defining features and a core reason behind its sustained success.

Alba was acutely aware that rapid growth can lead to compromises, especially when it involves scaling production, entering new markets, and meeting the demand for a broader product range. To ensure that Honest's commitment to safety and environmental responsibility remained a priority, she took an active role in overseeing product development and quality control. From the start, Honest's products were formulated without harmful chemicals, artificial fragrances, or ingredients linked to health risks, and Alba was insistent that this would remain the standard even as the company scaled. She personally vetted ingredient lists and reviewed reports from testing labs, partnering with scientists and product developers who shared her passion for safe, clean ingredients. By staying directly involved in the details of product formulation, Alba was able to ensure that Honest's growth did not dilute its founding commitment to safety.

Alba also recognized that as Honest grew, so did the scrutiny surrounding its environmental claims and sustainability practices. She took proactive steps to ensure that the company's eco-friendly mission remained credible, emphasizing that expansion would not come at the expense of environmental responsibility. Honest committed to using recyclable materials for its packaging and sought to source ingredients from suppliers who adhered to sustainable practices. Alba worked closely with her supply chain team, carefully selecting partners who shared the company's environmental values. This extended beyond product ingredients to include ethical labor practices, ensuring that Honest's growth was rooted in integrity. Alba's insistence on working only with suppliers and manufacturers who adhered to these high standards helped Honest establish a reputation as a company that was willing to prioritize ethics over convenience or cost-cutting.

One of the key strategies Alba implemented to maintain brand integrity was creating a company culture deeply aligned with Honest's mission. As the company grew and hired more employees, she made it a priority to embed the values of transparency, honesty, and responsibility into the organization's culture. Alba believed that if employees genuinely believed in Honest's mission, they would be more likely to uphold these values in their work. She led by example, actively engaging with teams across the company, from product development to customer service, reinforcing the importance of quality and transparency. Employees were encouraged to speak up if they saw potential issues or areas where the company could improve, creating an open environment where brand integrity was a shared responsibility. This inclusive culture helped Honest navigate growth without losing sight of its original mission, as employees at every level felt a personal stake in upholding the values that set the company apart.

Honest's commitment to transparency played a critical role in maintaining brand integrity as it scaled. Alba recognized that growth inevitably invited scrutiny, with customers, media, and industry analysts looking closely at Honest's claims and practices. Rather than shying away from this attention, Alba embraced it, committing to a level of openness that was unusual for a company of Honest's size. When issues arose—whether it was a product recall or a question about ingredient sourcing— Alba and her team addressed them publicly, providing detailed explanations and outlining steps taken to resolve any concerns. This transparency was especially crucial in an era where consumers increasingly expect brands to be accountable. Alba's openness built trust with customers, showing that Honest was a brand that valued integrity over image.

Another way Alba preserved brand integrity was by actively engaging with Honest's customer base. She understood that Honest's success was built on trust, and she took customer feedback seriously, using it to guide the company's decision-making process. Through social media, surveys, and direct communication channels, Honest invited customers to share their experiences, ideas, and concerns. Alba herself often participated in these conversations, making it clear that Honest valued its customers' voices. This two-way dialogue ensured that Honest stayed attuned to the needs and expectations of its audience, allowing the company to refine products and address issues in real-time. By staying connected to her consumers, Alba was able to make decisions that were not only aligned with Honest's mission but also responsive to the people who trusted her brand.

Alba's emphasis on maintaining brand integrity was particularly visible in Honest's approach to marketing and advertising. While rapid growth often pressures companies to push bold claims or adopt aggressive advertising tactics, Alba was careful to ensure that Honest's marketing remained authentic and transparent. Honest's campaigns highlighted real customer stories, focusing on the brand's commitment to safety and sustainability rather than making exaggerated claims. Alba understood that authenticity was key to preserving Honest's reputation and insisted on keeping marketing messaging honest and straightforward, even if it meant moving more slowly than competitors who prioritized quick wins over long-term trust. This approach not only reinforced Honest's credibility but also resonated with consumers who were weary of conventional, high-pressure advertising.

As Honest ventured into new markets and introduced a diverse array of products, Alba continued to prioritize alignment with the company's founding values. When launching Honest Beauty, she made sure the new line adhered to the same standards of safety and sustainability that had defined Honest's earlier products. Expanding into the beauty industry presented unique challenges, as it was a highly competitive field with established players and specific regulatory requirements. However, Alba remained steadfast in her commitment to ethical production and transparency. She was involved in every stage of Honest Beauty's development, from ingredient selection to packaging design, ensuring that each product was a true reflection of Honest's values.

Maintaining brand integrity amid rapid growth required Alba to constantly make choices that aligned with Honest's mission, even when it was difficult or required trade-offs. She set a powerful example for her team by demonstrating that growth should not come at the expense of the company's core principles. This unwavering dedication to honesty, transparency, and ethical practices became a defining characteristic of The Honest Company. It helped the brand grow into a trusted name in the consumer goods industry and inspired other companies to consider the importance of integrity in their own operations.

In the end, Alba's commitment to maintaining brand integrity was central to The Honest Company's success. Her hands-on approach, transparency, and dedication to ethical practices showed that it was possible to scale a company without sacrificing its core values. By staying true to its mission, Honest not only achieved impressive growth but also redefined what consumers could expect from brands in terms of trust, accountability, and responsibility. Through her commitment to brand integrity, Jessica Alba demonstrated that a company founded on honesty could thrive in a competitive marketplace, proving that business growth and ethical principles could go hand in hand.

Chapter 7: Social Impact and Sustainability

Commitment to the Environment: How Honest Co. has worked to use eco-friendly materials and reduce its environmental footprint.

From its inception, The Honest Company made sustainability and environmental responsibility cornerstones of its mission, prioritizing eco-friendly materials and practices to reduce its environmental footprint. Jessica Alba recognized early on that Honest's success depended on its ability to offer safe, sustainable products for families while also protecting the planet. She believed that companies should not only create safe products but also ensure that the production and disposal of those products would be as gentle on the environment as possible. As a result, Honest set out to create a positive environmental impact across every aspect of its business—from product design to packaging, sourcing, and distribution. This commitment to sustainability has been instrumental in building Honest's reputation as an industry leader in responsible production and has helped foster a loyal customer base that values both product safety and environmental ethics.

Honest Co. began its sustainability journey by focusing on the materials used in its products, striving to incorporate renewable, biodegradable, and non-toxic ingredients. When formulating household and personal care items, the company avoided the use of harsh chemicals and instead relied on plant-based ingredients, sourced whenever possible from suppliers that adhered to environmentally friendly practices. Alba insisted that Honest's ingredient list exclude commonly used chemicals known to harm both people and the environment, such as parabens, sulfates, and phthalates. The result was a product line designed not only to be safe for consumers but also to minimize ecological harm. Additionally, Alba and her team ensured that Honest's suppliers were aligned with its eco-conscious goals, seeking partners who maintained sustainable farming practices and reduced pesticide use. By maintaining high standards for ingredient sourcing, Honest was able to ensure that each product's environmental impact was minimized from the ground up.

Packaging is often one of the most wasteful aspects of consumer products, and Honest Co. tackled this issue with an innovative approach, designing packaging that was both sustainable and user-friendly. Recognizing the high environmental cost of single-use plastics, Honest committed to using recyclable and biodegradable materials wherever possible. For instance, the company selected recyclable bottles, paper, and cardboard for packaging and actively worked to reduce plastic use in product containers. Alba and her team collaborated with packaging experts to design eco-friendly alternatives, even if it meant higher production costs. By making these choices, Honest Co. managed to divert considerable waste from landfills, encouraging customers to recycle and dispose of packaging responsibly. To increase consumer awareness, Honest also provided clear labeling on its packaging, guiding customers on how to recycle each component, and educating them on the environmental impact of proper disposal practices.

The Honest Company's dedication to reducing its carbon footprint extended beyond just product ingredients and packaging. The company also took steps to make its supply chain and manufacturing processes as sustainable as possible. Honest worked to source ingredients locally whenever possible to reduce the environmental costs of transportation. This approach not only lowered carbon emissions associated with long-distance shipping but also supported local economies and small suppliers who shared Honest's values. For its manufacturing facilities, Honest selected partners with a strong commitment to energy efficiency and waste reduction, ensuring that products were made in a manner that conserved resources. Honest has consistently evaluated its suppliers' environmental practices, choosing partners who prioritize clean energy and efficient manufacturing techniques, which significantly reduces greenhouse gas emissions. Alba's dedication to choosing eco-friendly suppliers set a new standard for sustainability in the consumer goods industry, pushing competitors to reconsider their environmental practices.

Honest Co. further demonstrated its environmental commitment through partnerships and certifications that underscored the company's dedication to sustainability. The company worked closely with third-party certification organizations, like the Environmental Working Group (EWG) and B Corporation, to verify the environmental responsibility of its products and operations. Earning B Corporation certification was a milestone for Honest Co., as it demonstrated that the company met rigorous standards of social and environmental performance, accountability, and transparency. This certification aligned with Alba's goal of creating a company that valued positive impact as much as profit. Alba's pursuit of B Corp certification was not just symbolic; it was a reflection of Honest's commitment to continuous improvement in sustainability and social responsibility.

Another innovative initiative by Honest Co. was its move toward a circular economy, particularly in product refill options and reusable packaging. Recognizing the environmental toll of single-use products, Honest developed refillable options for select products, allowing customers to purchase refills instead of new containers each time. This approach reduced plastic waste, encouraged consumers to embrace more sustainable habits, and contributed to the growing circular economy movement, which aims to reduce waste by reusing materials as much as possible. Honest's refill options became a popular choice for eco-conscious consumers, demonstrating that sustainable business practices can also serve as a unique selling point. The refill program further enhanced Honest's reputation as an innovative, eco-friendly brand, creating a loyal customer base that appreciated the company's genuine commitment to environmental care.

Honest's transparency about its sustainability goals has been instrumental in building trust with consumers who increasingly seek brands that take environmental responsibility seriously. Honest Co. maintains an open dialogue with its customers, sharing updates on its progress, areas for improvement, and new sustainability initiatives. This level of transparency has been particularly effective in an industry where consumers are often left in the dark about a brand's environmental practices.

Honest's dedication to clear communication has empowered customers to make informed decisions, fostering a sense of partnership and shared purpose in reducing environmental impact. Alba's willingness to acknowledge the challenges of sustainable production and her commitment to finding solutions have resonated with customers, who value her honesty and determination to lead by example.

Beyond its own operations, The Honest Company has used its platform to advocate for wider environmental change in the industry. Alba has frequently spoken out about the need for more rigorous regulations around product safety and environmental standards. She has advocated for policies that promote transparency, safe ingredients, and sustainable production practices, calling on other companies to follow Honest's lead. Alba's advocacy has helped raise awareness of environmental issues within the consumer goods industry and inspired other companies to consider sustainability as a core business value. By using her platform and influence, Alba has shown that businesses can lead by example, driving industry-wide change toward a more sustainable future.

In a business landscape where profitability often overshadows ecological responsibility, Honest Co.'s commitment to the environment is a testament to Alba's determination to create a brand that balances success with purpose. Her approach has proven that growth and sustainability can coexist and that consumers increasingly favor brands that prioritize the planet. Honest's initiatives to reduce its environmental footprint—from eco-friendly materials and packaging to responsible manufacturing practices—have not only set it apart as an industry leader but have also demonstrated the power of purpose-driven business. Through its ongoing dedication to sustainability, The Honest Company continues to show that protecting the planet and meeting consumer needs can be complementary goals, setting an inspiring example for brands around the world.

Making a Difference: Alba's broader social mission, including her work with charities, and Honest's community engagement and environmental partnerships.

Jessica Alba's influence goes well beyond the walls of The Honest Company, extending into meaningful social initiatives that reflect her deep commitment to community well-being, equity, and environmental justice. Alba has leveraged her personal brand and business success to amplify her social mission, collaborating with numerous charities, supporting underserved communities, and leading environmental efforts aimed at broader systemic change. The Honest Company, reflecting Alba's dedication, has embraced community engagement and environmental partnerships as core elements of its identity, enabling the company to make a tangible difference in the lives of individuals and communities. Alba's goal has always been to create a company that not only provides safe, high-quality products but also contributes positively to society, supporting sustainable, healthy communities. Her broader social mission is evident in her charitable work, as well as in Honest's strategic partnerships that address both environmental and social causes.

Alba's personal dedication to giving back is evident through her active involvement with several charitable organizations and her contributions to causes focused on children's health, education, and family well-being. As a mother, Alba feels a strong connection to causes that support children and families, and she's been a long-time advocate for organizations that promote these values. She's actively partnered with organizations such as Baby2Baby, which provides essentials like diapers, clothing, and school supplies to children living in poverty across the United States. Through her involvement, Alba has helped to amplify Baby2Baby's mission and has encouraged other high-profile figures to contribute to the cause, significantly increasing the organization's impact. Alba's work with Baby2Baby not only underscores her commitment to helping underserved families but also reflects the values that Honest Co. holds dear: caring for others, creating opportunities for children to thrive, and ensuring access to basic needs that promote dignity and health.

Beyond personal charity work, Alba has infused The Honest Company with a spirit of giving, making social responsibility an essential aspect of its operations. Honest Co. has consistently contributed to various causes, particularly those that support vulnerable families, improve public health, and promote environmental sustainability. For instance, the company has organized regular donations of products to families in need, partnering with local shelters, disaster relief efforts, and nonprofit organizations to ensure that essential goods reach those who need them most. This community-driven approach allows Honest Co. to actively support communities in crisis, such as during natural disasters or other emergencies. Additionally, Honest has committed to providing ongoing product donations to organizations that work with underserved communities, including women's shelters and low-income family support centers. These donations, often including items like baby products, personal care items, and cleaning supplies, are designed to ease the burden on families in need and highlight Honest's dedication to contributing to healthier, safer environments.

Alba and Honest Co. have also been vocal advocates for environmental justice, taking steps to address the systemic issues that disproportionately affect marginalized communities. In recognition of the fact that environmental hazards and pollution often impact low-income and minority communities the most, Honest has developed partnerships with organizations that aim to combat environmental inequities. One such partnership is with the Environmental Working Group (EWG), an organization that works to raise awareness about harmful chemicals in everyday products and advocate for stronger safety standards. Honest Co. shares EWG's commitment to transparency in product safety and has worked closely with them to advocate for stricter regulations in the consumer goods industry. Alba herself has been an outspoken supporter of regulatory reform, calling on lawmakers to enforce more rigorous testing and safety standards to protect vulnerable populations from exposure to toxic chemicals. By aligning with EWG and similar organizations, Honest Co. amplifies its impact, helping to promote healthier and safer environments for all.

The Honest Company's environmental partnerships are integral to its broader social mission, focusing on sustainable practices that benefit both people and the planet. In collaboration with sustainability-focused organizations, Honest Co. has supported initiatives aimed at reducing waste, conserving resources, and promoting responsible consumption. One of the company's most impactful partnerships has been with TerraCycle, a company known for its work in recycling difficult-to-recycle products and materials. Through this partnership, Honest has launched programs that allow customers to return empty product containers for recycling, significantly reducing landfill waste and encouraging a culture of reusability. This initiative not only demonstrates Honest's commitment to sustainability but also empowers its customers to participate in environmental stewardship. Alba has been a strong advocate for such programs, promoting the importance of a circular economy and encouraging other companies to follow suit in reducing waste through recycling and sustainable production practices.

Additionally, Honest Co. has collaborated with nonprofit organizations to address environmental education and climate change. Alba and her team believe that creating a lasting impact requires not only immediate action but also long-term education and awareness-building. To this end, Honest has supported programs that teach young people about environmental responsibility, sustainable practices, and the impact of their choices on the planet. By funding educational programs in schools and community centers, Honest Co. fosters a new generation of environmentally conscious individuals who are equipped to make informed decisions about their consumption habits. Alba views this as an essential part of Honest's mission, as she believes that empowering young people with knowledge is one of the most effective ways to create a sustainable future.

One of Honest Co.'s guiding principles is its dedication to transparency, which Alba sees as essential for building consumer trust and driving meaningful social impact. In line with this commitment, Honest has publicly shared its progress toward sustainability goals, including updates on eco-friendly initiatives, challenges, and future objectives. Alba has consistently pushed for this level of openness, understanding that consumers want to support brands that prioritize accountability and honesty. This transparent approach is central to Honest's community engagement efforts, as it allows customers and partners to see the company's dedication to its values, understand its impact, and feel connected to a shared mission. By regularly sharing progress reports and engaging in open dialogues with stakeholders, Honest has cultivated a supportive community that feels personally invested in the company's mission.

Alba's dedication to social causes, both through Honest Co. and her personal charitable work, illustrates her belief in the power of business to be a force for good. By prioritizing community engagement, supporting families in need, addressing environmental injustices, and advocating for safer, healthier products, Alba has turned Honest Co. into a company with a meaningful purpose that resonates with consumers around the world. Her broader social mission has transformed Honest from just a product-focused business into a true social enterprise—one that doesn't just serve customers but also strives to create a positive impact in the lives of individuals and communities alike. Through her work, Alba has demonstrated that a successful business can and should be part of a larger movement for social and environmental justice, setting a powerful example for others to follow.

Chapter 8: Lessons on Resilience and Reinvention

Personal Growth: Jessica's growth as a businesswoman, including balancing her family and business roles.

Jessica Alba's journey from actress to entrepreneur wasn't just about building a successful business—it was also a deeply personal transformation that required resilience, adaptability, and an unwavering commitment to her values. Balancing the demands of The Honest Company with her roles as a mother, wife, and public figure, Alba has demonstrated remarkable growth, both as a leader and as a person. Over the years, she has evolved from an industry outsider into a savvy businesswoman, driven by her dedication to providing safe products, and grounded by her commitment to her family and community. Her personal growth has been an integral part of Honest Co.'s success, shaping the company's mission, values, and vision in powerful ways.

When Alba first transitioned into the business world, she faced a steep learning curve. Coming from Hollywood, where the dynamics are vastly different, she had to master the nuances of entrepreneurship, from funding rounds to product development and marketing strategies. Alba has openly shared that this shift was challenging, requiring her to learn new skills and step outside her comfort zone. She enrolled in business courses, studied the consumer goods industry, and surrounded herself with advisors who could help guide her. This dedication to learning helped her gain the expertise she needed to make informed decisions and build a company that could compete with established brands. As Alba herself has said, "I didn't know everything, but I knew what I wanted, and I learned along the way." This openness to growth and commitment to knowledge has set her apart and made her a respected voice in the industry.

Balancing her ambitious career with her responsibilities as a mother has been one of the most significant and fulfilling aspects of Alba's personal journey. From the beginning, Alba's family has been the driving force behind her vision for The Honest Company, as it was her experience as a new mother that inspired her to create safer, healthier products. Alba's two daughters and son, along with her husband, have been central to her motivation and have influenced her approach to both business and life. She has often shared how important it is for her to be present for her family, to set an example of resilience and dedication, and to show her children the value of hard work, integrity, and purpose. While balancing her role as a CEO and mother has its challenges, Alba has created a supportive environment at Honest Co. that respects family time, recognizing that a successful business can and should allow space for family priorities.

Alba's journey as a business leader has also been a lesson in resilience. The Honest Company's path hasn't always been smooth; the company has faced numerous challenges, from legal issues to product recalls and public scrutiny. But Alba's response to these setbacks has shown how much she has grown as a businesswoman. Rather than shying away, she faced these obstacles head-on, leading with transparency, empathy, and a determination to improve. She has spoken about how these experiences have helped her develop a thicker skin, stronger problem-solving skills, and an understanding that failure is a natural part of growth. Her resilience has been a defining feature of her leadership, proving to her team and the world that she's fully committed to Honest Co.'s mission and values.

This growth has also influenced the way she leads her team. Alba has developed a management style that emphasizes collaboration, empathy, and empowerment. She has assembled a team of experts who share her commitment to Honest's values, and she works closely with them, encouraging open communication and mutual respect. Alba's inclusive approach fosters a culture where her team feels empowered to contribute ideas, share feedback, and take ownership of their work. This hands-on, supportive leadership style has not only contributed to the company's success but has also helped Alba grow as a leader, teaching her the importance of trust, delegation, and adaptability.

As Honest Co. has expanded, Alba has had to manage the increasing demands of her role, yet she remains dedicated to striking a balance between her personal and professional life. She often talks about the importance of self-care, setting boundaries, and finding time to recharge—lessons she has learned as she juggled multiple roles. Alba is a strong advocate for prioritizing health and wellness, and she practices what she preaches, incorporating healthy habits and mindfulness practices into her daily routine. She also emphasizes the value of community support, leaning on her family, friends, and team members to help her maintain balance. This holistic approach has allowed Alba to thrive as a mother and CEO, showing that success doesn't have to come at the expense of personal well-being.

Jessica Alba's personal growth has been a powerful driver of The Honest Company's success. Through her journey, she has proven that a celebrity can transition into business not just with flair, but with substance, authenticity, and a commitment to making a positive impact. Her ability to balance her roles as a mother, entrepreneur, and public figure has inspired many, illustrating that personal growth and professional achievement are intertwined. Alba's evolution from Hollywood starlet to business mogul isn't just a story of success; it's a testament to her resilience, integrity, and unwavering commitment to creating a better world for her family, her customers, and future generations.

What Success Means: Her redefinition of success beyond profits, focusing on impact, family, and health.

For Jessica Alba, success is not defined solely by sales figures or market dominance. While The Honest Company has achieved remarkable financial milestones, Alba's personal concept of success goes far beyond profits, centering instead on meaningful impact, family, and health. In an industry where shareholder returns often overshadow purpose, Alba has redefined what it means to succeed by staying committed to her original mission: to create safe, eco-friendly products that improve lives and leave a positive footprint on the planet.

Alba's focus on impact is evident in every facet of The Honest Company, from the careful sourcing of materials to ethical manufacturing processes. She has always envisioned her company as a force for good, a brand that prioritizes people and the environment. For Alba, success lies in making a real difference in the lives of customers— helping parents find peace of mind in using products that are safe for their families and the planet. Her company's commitment to transparency and sustainability reflects her belief that success means being responsible stewards of the Earth, ensuring that the impact Honest leaves behind is one of care, respect, and improvement.

This idea of impact goes beyond her brand's products to include Honest's broader social mission. Alba has been an advocate for community involvement, engaging her company in partnerships with charities, social initiatives, and environmental organizations. She sees Honest as part of a larger movement toward corporate responsibility, aiming to show that a successful company can—and should—contribute positively to the world. By aligning the company's goals with societal needs, Alba has built a brand that speaks to consumers who also value purpose-driven choices, further cementing her belief that true success is achieved by enriching the lives of others.

At the core of Alba's redefinition of success is her family, a source of inspiration and grounding for her. Her children and family were the reasons she pursued a safer, cleaner product line, and they continue to remind her of what truly matters. For Alba, success means being able to make a positive impact in her professional life without sacrificing her role as a mother and partner. She has often shared how important it is for her to set an example of hard work and resilience for her children, demonstrating that it's possible to pursue one's dreams while staying committed to family. Balancing the demands of running a growing company with the responsibilities of motherhood has become a core part of her life philosophy, teaching her that true success is found in harmonizing work with the joy and meaning that family brings.

Health, too, is a pillar of her view on success. Driven by her own health challenges and inspired by the desire to protect her children from harmful chemicals, Alba has placed health at the center of her life and her company's mission. She has created a brand that reflects her dedication to wellness, promoting products that prioritize safety and well-being over shortcuts and profits. For Alba, success means nurturing a lifestyle of balance and mindfulness, one that respects the body, values self-care, and encourages others to prioritize their own health and happiness. This holistic approach to wellness, integrated into Honest Co.'s product philosophy and her personal life, underscores her belief that health is foundational to a fulfilling life and a successful career.

In the end, Jessica Alba's success is not just about building a billion-dollar brand but about shaping a legacy that values impact, integrity, and a balance between work and family. Her journey from Hollywood to the boardroom is a testament to her belief that success is multi-dimensional, encompassing purpose, connection, and well-being. Through her company, Alba has challenged the traditional definition of success, showing that profits can follow when a brand is built on genuine values and a deep commitment to making a difference. For Jessica Alba, success means leaving a legacy of positive impact, nurturing her family, and prioritizing health—all while remaining true to the values that set her on this path in the first place.

Chapter 9: Honest Advice for Aspiring Entrepreneurs

Advice on Building a Purpose-Driven Business: Jessica's tips for entrepreneurs who want to build with integrity and social responsibility.

Jessica Alba's journey from Hollywood to the entrepreneurial world is a powerful example of building a business with purpose at its core. For entrepreneurs aiming to create brands that not only succeed financially but also make a meaningful impact, Alba's insights provide a valuable guide. Her advice focuses on building with authenticity, staying grounded in values, and keeping the customer's well-being at the forefront—all of which have shaped The Honest Company into a purpose-driven brand that resonates with consumers. Here are some of her essential tips for those looking to build a business with integrity and social responsibility:

Start with a Mission that Matters

Alba's first piece of advice to entrepreneurs is to begin with a mission that deeply resonates. For her, The Honest Company was born from a personal need and desire to create safe, non-toxic products for her family. She encourages aspiring entrepreneurs to ask themselves what problem they truly want to solve and to build their business around that solution. "When your mission is meaningful to you personally," she says, "it keeps you going when things get tough." A purpose-driven mission gives a business a strong foundation and helps set it apart, fostering an emotional connection with customers who share that mission.

Understand and Listen to Your Customer

Alba emphasizes the importance of truly understanding the needs and values of your target audience. For her, listening to consumers has been crucial, helping her shape The Honest Company's offerings to align with what people actually want and need. She suggests connecting directly with potential customers, conducting research, and staying open to feedback. Building a purpose-driven brand means prioritizing customers' well-being over profit and being transparent and responsive to their concerns. Alba explains, "At the end of the day, our customers are our best guides in shaping the brand."

Prioritize Integrity Over Shortcuts

In an industry where quick gains and shortcuts are often tempting, Alba advises entrepreneurs to stay committed to integrity, even when the path is more challenging. She recalls numerous moments when The Honest Company faced pressures to compromise on ingredients, sourcing, or transparency for the sake of cost or speed. Alba's commitment to maintaining high standards has helped Honest Co. build a reputation of trust with consumers, and she believes that upholding integrity is essential for long-term success. "Integrity is the backbone of a purpose-driven business," she explains. "It's about making choices that you'll be proud of, no matter what."

Build with a Long-Term Vision

Purpose-driven companies require a vision that goes beyond immediate profits. Alba encourages entrepreneurs to think about the legacy they want to leave behind and to align their decisions with that long-term impact. For her, Honest Co. was about creating a healthier world for her children and future generations. She stresses that building with longevity in mind allows a business to weather challenges and evolve while staying true to its mission. A clear, long-term vision also serves as a compass, helping guide decisions and inspire team members who are motivated by a shared goal.

Surround Yourself with a Team that Shares Your Values

Alba's advice to entrepreneurs is to bring on team members who are passionate about the company's mission and align with its core values. A purpose-driven business can only thrive if everyone within the company believes in the vision and works towards it together. Alba speaks of her commitment to creating a culture at The Honest Company that values transparency, collaboration, and purpose, which has enabled the team to stay motivated and resilient. "When you're surrounded by people who care about the same things, it creates a powerful energy that drives the business forward," she says.

Embrace Transparency and Learn from Setbacks

Alba has always been open about the challenges Honest Co. has faced, from product recalls to legal issues. Her advice to other entrepreneurs is to embrace transparency when things go wrong and to use setbacks as opportunities to improve. Being open and honest with customers builds trust and shows a commitment to improvement. Alba emphasizes that facing challenges with integrity not only strengthens the brand but also serves as a powerful lesson in resilience for the team. "Mistakes are part of the journey," she shares. "What matters is how you respond to them and what you learn along the way."

Stay Grounded in Your Personal "Why"

For Alba, her family has always been her "why"—the reason she started The Honest Company and the motivation that keeps her going. She advises entrepreneurs to stay grounded in their personal purpose, the core reason they began their journey, as it can sustain them through difficult times. A strong "why" can remind entrepreneurs of the larger picture, helping them push through obstacles while remaining committed to their mission. "When you know your why, you can overcome any challenge," Alba says. "It keeps you focused and resilient."

In building a purpose-driven business, Jessica Alba's advice reveals that success is not just about what you create but about how and why you create it. By focusing on integrity, long-term vision, and authenticity, she has crafted a brand that stands for something bigger than itself—a company that improves lives, respects the planet, and aligns with her values. For Alba, creating a business with purpose means staying true to her mission, her customers, and herself, and she encourages all entrepreneurs to do the same.

Maintaining Authenticity: How to stay true to your brand and your audience, even as you grow and adapt.

For any business, growth and adaptation are essential to stay relevant and competitive. However, expanding without compromising your brand's core values and maintaining an authentic connection with your audience can be a challenge. Jessica Alba's journey with The Honest

Company is a powerful example of how to scale a brand while staying true to its original mission and identity. Here are insights on how to maintain authenticity, connect with your audience, and remain grounded in your brand's purpose, even as you navigate growth.

Stay Connected to Your Original Mission

One of the cornerstones of authenticity is remembering why you started in the first place. Alba built The Honest Company to provide safe, eco-friendly products that parents could trust. She advises businesses to consistently revisit the core mission that sparked the brand's creation and make it a focal point of every expansion decision. Whether it's a new product line or a partnership, staying aligned with this mission helps ensure that growth decisions don't stray from the brand's purpose. "Our mission is our guiding light," she says, "and if we lose sight of that, we lose our authenticity." Grounding every decision in your original purpose helps your brand stay genuine in the eyes of your audience.

Prioritize Transparency in Every Stage

Transparency builds trust, especially as companies grow and make changes to adapt to market needs. Alba emphasizes the importance of being open with customers about your brand's choices and challenges, from ingredient sourcing to product development and partnerships. Honest Co. has maintained this openness, which has helped them create a loyal following. Alba's advice is to "bring your customers along on the journey" by sharing updates, explaining your decisions, and being upfront when issues arise. This transparency reinforces your brand's commitment to authenticity and builds a deeper, more resilient relationship with your audience.

Adapt Without Compromising Core Values

Growth often requires change, but change should not come at the expense of your brand's core values. When The Honest Company introduced new products, like beauty and skincare lines, Alba ensured that these expansions adhered to the same eco-friendly, health-conscious principles that defined their original offerings. For her, scaling didn't mean cutting corners or compromising quality but rather evolving in ways that still aligned with the brand's values. "It's okay to adapt," she explains, "as long as you're doing it in a way that's true to who you are." Ensuring that each new venture or product resonates with your brand's core values helps maintain consistency and authenticity, even as you expand.

Know Your Audience and Engage with Them Regularly

Authenticity requires a deep understanding of your audience's evolving needs, preferences, and values. Alba has emphasized the importance of actively listening to her customers, through both direct engagement and market research, to keep Honest Co. in tune with what matters most to them. Engaging regularly with your audience— whether through social media, feedback channels, or community events—helps maintain a close connection and shows that you value their input. Alba's advice to other entrepreneurs is to "treat your customers as collaborators in the journey," which creates a two-way relationship and ensures that your brand grows in ways that are meaningful to your audience.

Remain Personally Involved and Visible

Alba's hands-on approach has been key to The Honest Company's authentic identity. Despite the demands of running a large company, she has remained actively involved in product development, brand strategy, and public engagement. This personal involvement reinforces the brand's authenticity, showing customers that the person behind the company genuinely cares about its mission. For entrepreneurs, staying visible and engaged with both the team and the customer base helps to humanize the brand and convey authenticity. "Your audience needs to see that you're invested in the brand's growth and staying true to your vision," Alba explains.

Learn from Mistakes and Show Accountability

Alba has often faced challenges with The Honest Company, from product recalls to public criticism, and her approach has always been to handle these moments with transparency and accountability. She believes that mistakes are a part of the journey and that addressing them openly only strengthens a brand's authenticity. Acknowledging errors, apologizing when necessary, and committing to improvement show your audience that you are honest and committed to delivering on your promises. Alba's advice: "Don't be afraid of setbacks. Embrace them, learn from them, and show your audience that you're constantly striving to do better." This approach fosters loyalty and trust, key components of a brand's authenticity.

Empower a Team that Shares Your Values

A brand's authenticity is only as strong as the people behind it. Alba believes that building a team that genuinely believes in the company's mission is critical to maintaining authenticity as you grow. At The Honest Company, she has surrounded herself with people who are as committed to transparency, health, and sustainability as she is. Her advice to entrepreneurs is to hire and empower team members who embody your brand's values, ensuring that these values permeate every aspect of the company. When every team member is aligned with the mission, they become ambassadors of your brand's authenticity, helping to maintain its integrity at all levels.

Maintaining authenticity in the face of growth requires a commitment to your brand's core mission, values, and audience. By staying connected to these foundational elements, involving yourself personally, and fostering transparency, you can create a brand that resonates with genuine purpose. Jessica Alba's journey with The Honest Company shows that it's possible to scale while staying true to your original vision, proving that authenticity is not only a guiding principle but also a competitive advantage in today's market. For Alba, authenticity is about building a brand that reflects who she is and what she believes in, and she encourages all entrepreneurs to do the same as they grow and adapt.

Conclusion

Jessica's Legacy in Wellness and Business: Reflecting on her influence on the industry and the lasting impact of her dedication to creating change.

Jessica Alba's journey from Hollywood star to pioneering entrepreneur has left an indelible mark on both the wellness and business worlds. Her legacy isn't just about founding a successful company or achieving financial milestones; it's about transforming an industry that once sidelined health, safety, and sustainability in favor of profits. Through The Honest Company, she not only introduced consumers to safe, eco-friendly products but also challenged the industry to reevaluate its practices, proving that a commitment to wellness and social responsibility can go hand in hand with economic success.

Alba's dedication to transparency, integrity, and authenticity has redefined what it means to be a "celebrity entrepreneur." She didn't simply lend her name to a brand; she built one from the ground up, overcoming skepticism, product challenges, and the weight of high expectations. Her active involvement in every aspect of The Honest Company's development—from product innovation to environmental responsibility—showcases her unwavering commitment to the vision she set out to realize. This dedication has inspired a new generation of purpose-driven entrepreneurs and reshaped public perceptions about what is possible when passion is aligned with purpose.

In the wellness space, Jessica has emerged as a leader who cares deeply about the products she provides and the people who use them. Her influence extends far beyond the Honest label, impacting competitors and motivating other companies to adopt more transparent, health-conscious practices. She has shown that it's possible to thrive in business while being devoted to creating positive change, setting a new standard for companies everywhere to put people and the planet first.

As we look to the future, Jessica Alba's legacy will likely continue to shape industries far beyond wellness. She has proven that a business built with integrity and a focus on social good can inspire loyalty and create lasting impact. Her journey exemplifies the power of persistence, purpose, and passion, and her story will undoubtedly encourage others to think bigger, act with integrity, and pursue ventures that leave the world a better place. Through The Honest Company and her ongoing advocacy, Jessica Alba's influence endures—a reminder that meaningful change is possible when vision meets dedication.

Looking Forward: Where she and Honest Co. aim to go in the future and her vision for the wellness industry.

As Jessica Alba and The Honest Company look toward the future, their ambitions are firmly anchored in the core values that have shaped them: transparency, health, and sustainability. Jessica's vision goes beyond simply expanding Honest Co.'s product lines; she sees the brand as a catalyst for broader change in how businesses and consumers approach wellness, environmental responsibility, and ethical production. Her goal is to make wellness more accessible, safe, and sustainable for families around the world, leading the industry toward more accountable, people-centered practices.

In the coming years, Honest Co. aims to deepen its focus on innovation, exploring eco-conscious product advancements and seeking even cleaner, safer ingredients that set higher standards for quality and environmental impact. This may involve investing in green technologies that reduce packaging waste, prioritizing renewable resources, and developing formulas that are both effective and gentle on the planet. Jessica envisions Honest Co. as a leading example of how wellness and sustainability can be seamlessly integrated into everyday products without sacrificing effectiveness, comfort, or style.

Expanding Honest Co.'s global presence is also high on the agenda, with plans to reach new markets and cater to a more diverse, international audience. Jessica recognizes that wellness is a universal concern and that every family, regardless of location, deserves access to products they can trust. By prioritizing global growth, she hopes to extend Honest Co.'s impact, offering safe, eco-friendly solutions to households worldwide and creating a ripple effect of healthier lifestyles and mindful consumption on a global scale.

Looking at the wellness industry as a whole, Jessica foresees a shift toward greater accountability, where brands are not only expected to prioritize profit but also to protect consumers' well-being and the environment. She advocates for an industry where transparency and corporate responsibility are the norm, and where businesses engage openly with consumers, involving them in the journey toward healthier living. In her view, companies should be accountable not only for the products they sell but also for the ethical, environmental, and social impacts of their choices.

In the long term, Jessica hopes that Honest Co. will inspire other companies to rethink how they approach business. Her dream is to see an industry that emphasizes people and the planet just as much as profits—one where brands work together to raise standards, push for better regulations, and create positive social change. By leading Honest Co. into this new chapter, Jessica Alba envisions a future where her company continues to serve as a leader, innovator, and beacon of integrity, setting an example for the wellness industry and beyond.

Jessica's vision for Honest Co. is ambitious yet grounded in her original mission to bring honesty, safety, and health into households around the world. As both an entrepreneur and an advocate, she is committed to driving meaningful change in the industry and beyond, creating a legacy that inspires families, entrepreneurs, and companies alike to work toward a healthier, more sustainable future.

Chapter 10: "Lessons Learned: Insights for Aspiring Entrepreneurs"

Start with Purpose

The Power of a Mission-Driven Business

Jessica Alba's journey with The Honest Company was driven by her deep-rooted belief in creating safer, eco-friendly products for families. This commitment wasn't just a passing interest; it was the foundation of her brand, born from her own experiences with health issues and her desire to make a difference for families like her own.

Jessica's mission to provide clean, responsible products not only shaped her business vision but also acted as a steadfast guiding light during challenges. Whenever Honest Co. encountered setbacks—whether it was a product recall, public scrutiny, or market pressures—her dedication to this mission helped her persevere and stay focused.

Jessica's experience illustrates a powerful truth about mission-driven businesses: when a brand is founded on a genuine, impactful purpose, it provides entrepreneurs with a unique source of resilience. For Jessica, Honest Co. was never just about launching another product line. Her goal was to fill a gap in the market and raise the bar for product safety and sustainability. This mission gave her both motivation and a moral compass, ensuring that the brand never strayed from its values even as it grew.

Through Honest Co., Jessica underscores the importance of starting a business that's driven by a mission that resonates on a personal level. When a founder has an authentic connection to their brand's purpose, it creates a sense of fulfillment that goes beyond financial success and can sustain them through both the successes and the inevitable setbacks.

Creating Your Own Brand DNA

A strong mission doesn't just fuel the founder—it becomes the DNA of the entire company. From day one, Jessica understood that her vision for Honest Co. needed to be more than a tagline; it had to be woven into the fabric of the brand. This meant establishing clear, authentic values that would define every aspect of the company, from product development to customer interactions. Honest Co.'s commitment to transparency, safety, and eco-consciousness became its core principles, creating a distinct identity that customers could trust and recognize.

For aspiring entrepreneurs, Jessica offers valuable advice: take the time to define your brand's values early on, and ensure they are meaningful and authentic. These core values are more than just words; they influence the decisions you make, the people you hire, and the products you create. In Honest Co.'s case, the values of honesty, transparency, and eco-friendliness weren't just ideals—they became standards by which the brand operated, setting expectations for product quality, ingredient sourcing, and environmental responsibility.

Establishing a strong brand DNA helps shape a company's culture and guides product development. When Honest Co. expanded its product lines, each addition had to align with the company's commitment to safe, eco-friendly ingredients. By staying true to its values, Honest Co. was able to build a solid foundation of customer trust and loyalty. Consumers knew what to expect from the brand and understood that Honest Co. wasn't just another company capitalizing on trends; it was genuinely invested in creating products that aligned with its mission.

Jessica's approach highlights a key lesson: authenticity and consistency in brand values create long-term trust with consumers. By staying true to these values, Honest Co. didn't just create a brand—it built a community of like-minded people who shared its commitment to health, wellness, and environmental responsibility. For entrepreneurs, Jessica's experience serves as a reminder that building a meaningful brand starts with purpose and grows through authenticity, helping to establish a legacy that endures beyond the products themselves.

2. Build on Authenticity and Consistency

Being Transparent and Genuine

Jessica Alba knew from the outset that the success of The Honest Company would hinge on her ability to build an authentic brand. Unlike some celebrity-led ventures that rely heavily on star power without a solid foundation,

Honest Co. was driven by Jessica's genuine commitment to safer, eco-friendly products—a commitment born from her own health experiences and her desire to create a better future for her children. As she built Honest Co., Jessica made it her mission to align the brand's values with her personal beliefs, ensuring that every product reflected her dedication to transparency, integrity, and the well-being of customers and the planet.

Jessica didn't just put her name on a label; she was actively involved in shaping every facet of the company, from product design and materials to packaging and marketing. This hands-on approach allowed her to ensure that Honest Co. lived up to the standards she set for herself and for the brand. Her message to future entrepreneurs is clear: when building a brand, transparency and genuineness are non-negotiable. Customers today expect companies to be accountable, and they're quick to spot inauthenticity. Jessica's commitment to honesty, in both the brand's products and its communications, has earned Honest Co. a loyal customer base that trusts the brand's promises.

Balancing Personal Values with Market Needs

While Jessica's personal commitment to clean, safe products was at the heart of Honest Co., she also understood the importance of listening to her customers.

Jessica was mindful of the need to balance her vision with market demands, and this meant engaging with customers regularly to understand their needs, preferences, and concerns. From customer feedback sessions to extensive market research, she took steps to keep the brand in sync with what people truly wanted while staying true to her core values.

Jessica also embraced the importance of consistent communication in maintaining customer trust. She knew that Honest Co. had to be clear and transparent in all its messaging, from product labeling and ingredient sourcing to updates on new initiatives. This level of openness built credibility and reassured customers that Honest Co. would continue to prioritize safety and quality, even as it expanded into new markets and product categories. For Jessica, staying consistent in values and communication—even as the company grew—was essential in reinforcing the brand's authenticity.

Jessica's journey with Honest Co. highlights the powerful combination of authenticity and consistency in building a successful brand. For entrepreneurs, her approach offers an important lesson: by staying true to your mission, engaging genuinely with your customers, and consistently upholding your brand's values, you create a foundation of trust that resonates deeply with people. In Jessica's experience, authenticity isn't just a trend; it's the cornerstone of a brand that can thrive, evolve, and make a meaningful impact.

Listening to Customers

One of Jessica Alba's key philosophies in building The Honest Company was understanding her customers' real needs. From the beginning, Jessica recognized that listening to customers was essential to create products that genuinely addressed their concerns and fit their lifestyles. Rather than relying solely on market trends or assumptions, she invested time and resources in getting direct feedback, understanding her customer base, and adapting to their evolving expectations. Jessica's advice for entrepreneurs is simple but essential: connect with your customers early and often. Whether through social media, surveys, focus groups, or direct interactions, making a consistent effort to hear what customers have to say helps guide product development and fosters a sense of connection that customers value.

Gathering Honest Feedback

Creating an honest feedback loop is a powerful way to show customers that their voices are heard. Jessica emphasizes the importance of building transparency into every step of the feedback process. Honest Co. actively sought customer opinions through surveys, online reviews, and customer service channels. By encouraging customers to share their real experiences—both positive and negative—Jessica not only identified areas of improvement but also reinforced the company's commitment to transparency and accountability. For entrepreneurs, gathering honest feedback means welcoming constructive criticism as much as praise. Jessica's experience highlights that customers appreciate companies that value their input, creating stronger loyalty and trust in the long run.

Creating Products that Genuinely Address Consumer Needs

Jessica knew that building a brand with a mission required more than just promoting the concept; it meant creating products that made a real difference in customers' lives. Honest Co. was driven by the goal of providing safe, eco-friendly products that filled a genuine gap in the market, particularly for parents and health-conscious consumers. Jessica's practical advice for entrepreneurs is to focus on creating solutions that respond to real customer needs rather than on pushing out products for the sake of growth. By rooting product development in actual customer insights, businesses can build offerings that resonate on a deeper level, ensuring long-term relevance and loyalty.

For Jessica, building a meaningful brand is about more than just transactions; it's about connection. By listening attentively, encouraging open feedback, and staying committed to addressing consumer needs, she was able to create a brand that people feel invested in and loyal to. Her journey with Honest Co. shows that when you prioritize understanding and serving your customers, you build a foundation for sustainable growth and enduring impact.

3. Resilience and Learning from Mistakes

Overcoming Setbacks Gracefully

For Jessica Alba, the journey of building The Honest Company was not without its share of significant hurdles. Despite Honest Co.'s success, there were times when she faced setbacks that could have easily derailed her mission. Product recalls, legal challenges, and public scrutiny tested her resolve, and each challenge required an immense amount of resilience and focus on her part. One of the company's most public setbacks came when Honest Co. faced a product recall due to quality concerns, leading to negative media attention and skepticism from consumers who had once trusted the brand implicitly.

Rather than focusing on image management or dismissing the issue, Jessica leaned into problem-solving, placing customer trust and product integrity above all else. She took accountability, working closely with her team to investigate the cause and prevent future incidents. By addressing the issue transparently and focusing on how to make things right, she demonstrated that setbacks can be managed with grace and commitment to improvement. She prioritized rebuilding trust by directly engaging with customers, communicating openly about the changes Honest Co. was making, and reinforcing her commitment to safe, reliable products. This experience underlined her belief that a genuine, mission-driven approach could carry her brand through even the most challenging times.

Jessica's approach to setbacks highlights a valuable lesson for entrepreneurs: when faced with difficulties, it's essential to prioritize integrity and solutions over optics. Her transparency helped maintain customer loyalty and strengthened Honest Co.'s credibility. Instead of shying away from mistakes, she embraced the opportunity to improve, turning each obstacle into a stepping stone for a stronger, more reliable brand.

Embracing a Growth Mindset

Jessica's journey also showcases the importance of a growth mindset in entrepreneurship. Rather than seeing mistakes as failures, she viewed them as critical learning moments that ultimately strengthened both herself and her business. Jessica knew that challenges were inevitable, and instead of letting setbacks define her, she approached each one as an opportunity to grow. Her willingness to acknowledge mistakes, adjust, and keep moving forward reflects a belief in continuous improvement that defines resilient leaders.

In the fast-paced world of consumer products, Honest Co. needed to keep up with evolving consumer demands and industry standards, which sometimes meant making tough decisions and admitting when the company didn't get it right. This mindset allowed Jessica to view challenges as temporary and to push her team to find innovative solutions. Each setback provided her with insight into what her customers needed and where her brand could improve, helping her shape Honest Co. into a company that truly reflected her values and goals.

For Jessica, maintaining a growth mindset meant focusing on long-term goals over short-term fixes. By valuing learning over perfection, she ensured that Honest Co. continued to evolve and meet customer needs without losing its foundational principles. This resilience became a core part of the brand's identity, showing customers that Honest Co. was willing to learn, adapt, and improve to better serve them.

Jessica's experience is a testament to the power of resilience and a growth mindset in entrepreneurship. Mistakes are an inevitable part of building a business, but resilient entrepreneurs see failures as valuable experiences that lead to growth. By viewing each challenge as a learning opportunity and prioritizing customer trust and product quality, Jessica turned setbacks into building blocks for a stronger, more impactful brand. Her journey serves as an inspiring reminder to aspiring entrepreneurs: embrace your mistakes, learn from them, and use them as fuel to grow and evolve.4. Becoming a Lifelong Learner

Learning Business Basics: For Jessica, moving from entertainment into business required a commitment to learning about manufacturing, supply chains, marketing, and more. She could encourage aspiring entrepreneurs to be proactive learners, continually seeking knowledge in areas that are outside their expertise.

Seeking out Mentorship and Guidance: How Jessica surrounded herself with people who had skills she lacked and built a network of mentors and advisors. Practical tips on finding mentors, asking the right questions, and knowing when to listen to experienced voices.

5. Finding the Right Team and Partners

Building a Values-Aligned Team

Jessica Alba understood from the start that if The Honest Company was to succeed in its mission to deliver safe, eco-friendly products, she would need a team that shared her dedication to those values. For Jessica, hiring was never just about finding people with the right skills—it was about building a community of passionate, mission-driven individuals who believed in Honest's purpose. She knew that brand integrity could only be preserved if everyone on the team was genuinely committed to creating products that customers could trust and promoting transparency, safety, and environmental responsibility. Jessica was deliberate in her hiring process, prioritizing candidates who not only had relevant expertise but who also aligned with the company's core values.

To cultivate this values-aligned team, Jessica often looked for individuals with a proven interest in sustainable practices, consumer safety, and ethical business. She also emphasized the importance of transparency within the company, encouraging her team members to be open, collaborative, and accountable. By fostering a culture that celebrated shared values, Jessica built a team that didn't just work for Honest Co. but was invested in its mission. The team's commitment to the brand's principles allowed Honest Co. to grow without compromising its founding vision, even as the company expanded into new product lines and markets.

For entrepreneurs looking to create values-aligned teams, Jessica's experience highlights the importance of clearly defining the brand's mission and embedding it into the hiring and onboarding processes. Hiring individuals who are passionate about the mission creates a resilient foundation, ensuring that the company's principles remain at the forefront of decision-making, innovation, and customer interactions.

Choosing Investors and Partners Wisely

When it came to securing funding and selecting business partners, Jessica was just as discerning. She was well aware that not every investor or partner would fully understand or support Honest Co.'s mission. Instead of choosing investors solely for their financial backing, Jessica focused on finding people who believed in Honest's vision and were willing to support it wholeheartedly, even through challenges. Jessica knew that mission-driven companies often face unique obstacles, and she needed partners who would remain committed to the brand's goals, not just its profitability.

Finding the right investors was a challenging but rewarding process. Jessica engaged in thorough discussions to understand potential investors' values, their expectations, and their understanding of Honest Co.'s purpose. By aligning with investors who valued safe, eco-friendly products as much as she did, she was able to build a supportive network that provided more than just financial support—it offered guidance, patience, and shared enthusiasm for the company's mission.

Jessica's experience illustrates the importance of patience and discernment when choosing investors and partners. She encourages entrepreneurs to ask questions about potential investors' long-term vision, their previous investments, and how they've handled difficult times with other companies. Building a business with mission-aligned investors and partners can make all the difference, as it ensures that your support network is invested not only in your success but also in your purpose.

By building a values-aligned team and selecting supportive, mission-driven partners, Jessica Alba created a strong foundation for The Honest Company. Her approach to collaboration and partnership underscores the power of integrity in business, demonstrating that aligning with people who believe in your mission can help a company thrive through both successes and setbacks.

6. Growing with Integrity

Staying True to the Mission Amidst Growth

For Jessica Alba and The Honest Company, growth was never about expansion for expansion's sake. From the start, Jessica knew that her commitment to creating safe, eco-friendly products would set her company apart, and staying true to that mission was non-negotiable, even as Honest Co. experienced rapid demand and new opportunities for market entry. She recognized the importance of maintaining product quality and ethical standards, resisting the temptation to cut corners or compromise on materials as production scaled up. The process often meant facing tough decisions and choosing longer, more costly routes to ensure Honest's standards were met. For Jessica, every product had to live up to the brand's promise, regardless of how quickly the company was growing.

Jessica's commitment to quality meant that Honest Co. invested heavily in research, sustainable sourcing, and product testing, even as they launched new product lines. This approach not only preserved the integrity of each product but also reinforced customer trust. For aspiring entrepreneurs, Jessica's experience serves as a reminder that growth should never come at the expense of quality or principles. Staying true to the company's mission and core values, even in the face of challenges, creates a brand that customers can respect and rely on, which is crucial for long-term success.

Making Positive Impact Part of the Business Model

From the outset, Jessica's vision for Honest Co. extended beyond profits; she wanted the brand to make a real, positive impact on people's lives and the environment. By integrating social responsibility into the core of the business model, Honest Co. has created products that promote both personal wellness and environmental sustainability. For Jessica, making a positive impact was not an afterthought or a secondary benefit—it was a foundational part of how the company operated. This dedication to impact shaped decisions in product design, packaging, and sourcing, ensuring that each choice aligned with the brand's mission.

Jessica structured Honest Co.'s business model to reflect these values in a meaningful way. For example, she focused on using eco-friendly materials, reducing waste, and contributing to community projects that promoted health and safety. Honest Co. also engaged in partnerships with organizations that share similar goals, amplifying the company's positive impact. Jessica believes that by embedding social and environmental values into the business model itself, a brand can deliver value to its customers while also creating a lasting, positive legacy.

For entrepreneurs, Jessica's advice is to think strategically about how to weave impact into every aspect of the business. She suggests setting clear impact goals early on and structuring the business in a way that supports those goals consistently, whether through sustainable sourcing, community initiatives, or educational campaigns. By doing so, businesses can create a brand that doesn't just generate profit but actively contributes to a better world. Jessica's journey with Honest Co. shows that when a business grows with integrity, it becomes more than just a company—it becomes a movement that inspires customers and contributes to positive change.

7. Advice for the Next Generation of Entrepreneurs

Daring to Challenge the Norm

Jessica Alba's journey with The Honest Company stands as proof that some of the most impactful businesses are built on the courage to question the status quo. In an industry where many companies were content with conventional approaches and familiar formulas, Jessica took a different path, pushing boundaries to create products that prioritized consumer safety, transparency, and sustainability. Her message to future entrepreneurs is simple yet powerful: don't be afraid to disrupt traditional practices, especially in fields that are deeply personal to people's health, well-being, and the planet's future. When Jessica launched Honest Co., she challenged longstanding industry norms that ignored the health impacts of ingredients or overlooked the need for sustainable practices. This willingness to break from the ordinary laid the foundation for a brand that people could trust and one that set new standards in consumer products.

Jessica's advice to young entrepreneurs is to embrace this spirit of challenging the norm. Instead of conforming to established ways of doing business, she encourages them to ask difficult questions, to innovate fearlessly, and to explore new methods that address the gaps in today's market. For Jessica, true innovation comes from daring to address what others may ignore and offering consumers meaningful alternatives that prioritize well-being and ethical standards. By questioning the status quo and exploring unconventional solutions, entrepreneurs can drive real change and create brands that resonate deeply with today's conscious consumers.

Commitment to Lasting Impact

Jessica believes that the real measure of success extends far beyond profits. While financial success is important, her ultimate goal with The Honest Company has always been to create a brand that leaves a lasting, positive impact. For Jessica, success means knowing that her products have made a meaningful difference in people's lives by offering them safer choices and supporting a healthier environment. She has continually strived to build a company that stands as a force for good, a company that consumers can trust to uphold its mission no matter how much it grows.

In closing, Jessica's advice to the next generation of entrepreneurs centers on building something that matters—a business that is not only profitable but also meaningful, authentic, and responsible. She encourages them to approach their ventures with a strong sense of purpose and to keep impact at the core of their decisions. Jessica's vision for the future is filled with businesses that aren't just focused on immediate gains but are driven by the potential to make the world a better place. By committing to a mission that creates lasting impact, future entrepreneurs can forge a legacy that not only reflects their personal values but inspires future generations to carry forward the torch of positive change.

Commitment to Lasting Impact: Jessica could end the chapter with her vision of success not just as financial profitability but as making a meaningful, positive difference.

Being Transparent and Genuine

Jessica Alba knew from the outset that the success of The Honest Company would hinge on her ability to build an authentic brand. Unlike some celebrity-led ventures that rely heavily on star power without a solid foundation,

Honest Co. was driven by Jessica's genuine commitment to safer, eco-friendly products—a commitment born from her own health experiences and her desire to create a better future for her children. As she built Honest Co., Jessica made it her mission to align the brand's values with her personal beliefs, ensuring that every product reflected her dedication to transparency, integrity, and the well-being of customers and the planet.

Jessica didn't just put her name on a label; she was actively involved in shaping every facet of the company, from product design and materials to packaging and marketing. This hands-on approach allowed her to ensure that Honest Co. lived up to the standards she set for herself and for the brand. Her message to future entrepreneurs is clear: when building a brand, transparency and genuineness are non-negotiable. Customers today expect companies to be accountable, and they're quick to spot inauthenticity. Jessica's commitment to honesty, in both the brand's products and its communications, has earned Honest Co. a loyal customer base that trusts the brand's promises.

Balancing Personal Values with Market Needs

While Jessica's personal commitment to clean, safe products was at the heart of Honest Co., she also understood the importance of listening to her customers.

Jessica was mindful of the need to balance her vision with market demands, and this meant engaging with customers regularly to understand their needs, preferences, and concerns. From customer feedback sessions to extensive market research, she took steps to keep the brand in sync with what people truly wanted while staying true to her core values.

Jessica also embraced the importance of consistent communication in maintaining customer trust. She knew that Honest Co. had to be clear and transparent in all its messaging, from product labeling and ingredient sourcing to updates on new initiatives. This level of openness built credibility and reassured customers that Honest Co. would continue to prioritize safety and quality, even as it expanded into new markets and product categories. For Jessica, staying consistent in values and communication— even as the company grew—was essential in reinforcing the brand's authenticity.

Jessica's journey with Honest Co. highlights the powerful combination of authenticity and consistency in building a successful brand. For entrepreneurs, her approach offers an important lesson: by staying true to your mission, engaging genuinely with your customers, and consistently upholding your brand's values, you create a foundation of trust that resonates deeply with people. In Jessica's experience, authenticity isn't just a trend; it's the cornerstone of a brand that can thrive, evolve, and make a meaningful impact.

A Legacy of Purpose:

Redefining Success in Business and Beyond

In reflecting on Jessica Alba's journey from Hollywood to the helm of a billion-dollar company, we see a story that defies conventional narratives of celebrity success. The Honest Company wasn't just an entrepreneurial venture; it was a mission-driven response to Jessica's personal quest for safer, eco-friendly products, inspired by her own health challenges and commitment to family. This deep sense of purpose has been her guiding light, shaping each phase of the company's evolution and redefining what success means to her—beyond profits, market dominance, or fame.

Throughout her journey, Jessica stayed true to the values that formed the core of Honest Co.: transparency, integrity, and sustainability. This book has explored the triumphs and setbacks that came with building a brand that championed these values, often in an industry resistant to change. From the challenge of overcoming "celebrity brand" skepticism to dealing with product recalls and legal issues, Jessica demonstrated resilience, a growth mindset, and a willingness to learn. She saw each challenge as an opportunity for growth, illustrating that building an impactful business requires both courage and flexibility.

We've delved into how Jessica built a team that mirrored her mission, worked with partners who understood her long-term vision, and prioritized customers by listening to their feedback. We also saw how Jessica redefined what a "businesswoman" could be—authentic, values-driven, and willing to challenge industry norms to bring meaningful change. For Jessica, the growth of Honest Co. was always intertwined with making a positive impact, both in the lives of customers and on the environment, proving that business and social responsibility can be inseparable.

Ultimately, Jessica's story offers aspiring entrepreneurs a new model of success: one rooted in integrity, authenticity, and a lasting commitment to making a difference. As she looks to the future, Jessica's legacy will continue to influence the wellness and sustainability industries, showing that the most impactful businesses are those with a purpose greater than profit. For Jessica, success is measured not only by growth but by the positive change she leaves behind—a vision that invites the next generation to redefine their own paths in business and beyond.

www.ingramcontent.com/pod-product-compliance
Lightning Source LLC
Chambersburg PA
CBHW071514220526
45472CB00003B/1028